The
Great Walks
of
Europe

THE
GREAT WALKS
OF
EUROPE

RICHARD SALE

FRANCES LINCOLN LIMITED
PUBLISHERS

Frances Lincoln Limited
4 Torriano Mews
Torriano Avenue
London NW5 2RZ
www.franceslincoln.com

Designed by Carreg Limited, Ross-on-Wye, Herefordshire.

Printed and bound in China
9 8 7 6 5 4 3 2 1

Captions for the images in the preliminary and section opening pages:

Page 1	The Matterhorn in summer, Switzerland
Page 2-3	MacGillicuddy's Reeks, Ireland
Page 4-5	Sunrise, Corsica
Page 6-7	Zugspitze, Via Alpina
Page 8-9	Looking west over Serrato
Page 28-29	Refuge des Sarradets and the Cirque de Gavarnie
Page 54-55	Calenzana and the peaks near Monte Grosso
Page 70-71	Mont Blanc from Le Brévent
Page 92-93	The Eiger, Mönch and Jungfrau from the Schilthorn
Page 114-15	Aerial view east down the Reintal
Page 136-7	Aerial view of the high peaks of the Stubai
Page 152-3	Cimon della Pala from Cima Rosetta
Page 172-3	The Devil's Punchbowl
Page 196-7	MacGillicuddy's Reeks across Lough Acoose
Page 218-19	Buachaille Etive Mòr and the entrance to Glencoe
Page 238-9	Aerial view of Kebnekaise and the Rabots Glacier, with Drakryggen (Dragonsback) to the left
Page 254	The Snowdon Horseshoe across Llynau Mymbyr, Wales

CONTENTS

Long Walks

Day Walks

INTRODUCTION

Exactly when the first long-distance footpath – that is, a trail which takes days rather than hours to complete – was created is a matter for debate to be enjoyed at the end of a day's walking. In the last decade of the eighteenth century French coastguards created new paths and linked existing ones along Brittany's coast in an effort to stop, or at least minimize, the smuggling trade. Such a professional interest in walking might not seem an appropriate starting point for what is now a major outdoor activity, and it is almost certainly the case that, in the following century, groups of walking enthusiasts were linking footpaths to produce more demanding outings. In the USA the Appalachian Trail was conceived in the early years of the twentieth century, and that initiative was rapidly taken up by walkers throughout Europe. It was not, though, until the post-war years that amateur enthusiasm was taken up in any concerted official way. In 1947 the French formed an association whose aim was to create and maintain Grande Randonnées (GR), a series of 'great excursions' which sought out the best the landscape had to offer. In a salute to the ancient history of the trails, one walk, GR34, followed the old coastguard path around the coast of Brittany.

France's initiative was taken up by other European countries and a network of walks was soon established across the Continent, many linked at national borders so that walkers could pursue their enthusiasm from country to country. Although these European-wide walks were initially no more than notional, they have become official, at first with the establishment of 'E' routes, and more recently with the creation of the Via Alpina series, a marvellous concept which links mountain GRs so that the committed walker can thread a route across the European Alps from Slovenia to France.

This book sets down a selection of these long-distance trails. Every walker will, of course, have an opinion on which are the best, the 'great walks', but few will argue that the ones selected are among the finest. In the main they seek out wonderful landscapes, from the high Alps to the wilderness of Arctic Sweden and the pastoral delights of south-western Ireland. But they do not ignore history, taking in a route that has a claim to being the oldest in Europe, England's Ridgeway.

For many, time and other constraints mean that the completion of a GR in a single trek will remain an aspiration. I hope what they find here will inspire them to complete one of the longer walks in stages. But for some even that idea may not be a possibility, and for them, interspersed among the GRs are a series of some of Europe's finest day walks, the selection again including magnificent, sometimes challenging, landscapes, but also offering less arduous outings.

GR7

SPAIN

Many people, when queried about the highest mountain in Spain, will suggest a Pyrénéan peak. But the answer is actually well removed from the Pyrénées, almost as far removed as it is possible to be. Mulhacén (11,421ft/3,482m), named for the Moorish king Muley Al Hassan, rises in the Sierra Nevada, a range of peaks (formed by the same tectonic process that uplifted the Alps, and also comprising a range of rocks, chiefly metamorphic gneisses and micaschists, but including dolomitic limestone) that includes two dozen (well, twenty-three) tops of over 9,840ft (3,000m). The Sierra Nevada lies in Andalucía, a region of Spain more famous for the beaches of the Costa del Sol, for Málaga and Marbella, and, inland, for the cities of Seville, Granada and Córdoba. These names talk of sunny weather and high temperatures, while European mountains of around 10,000ft (3,048m) are more often associated with snow and winter sports. The Sierra Nevada offers both: summer temperatures that can reach 104°F/40°C in the valleys and the high 60s°F/low 20s°C on the summits, and skiing in winter. The range is a relatively compact rectangle of upland, much broader west–east than it is north–south, and with few spectacular peaks, appearing more as an elevated plateau; walkers head west or east following a broad, undulating ridge.

Apart from a National Park and a number of Natural Parks, set up to protect areas of outstanding beauty, the region is rich in unspoilt or largely agricultural landscapes. As the last area of Spain to have been occupied by the Moors, Andalucía is historically interesting. It is also famed for its collection of whitewashed villages, often perched on top, or on the side, of a hill. Gleaming in the sun the villages are a joy to see from a distance, and when you reach them they are equally attractive, often with fine restaurants serving local cuisine, and craft shops, the latter usually including at least one selling leatherwork. Some of the more attractive villages, the Pueblos Blancos, are on routes devised by the region's tourist authorities.

Given this plethora of worthwhile sites and landscapes, it is no surprise to discover that that the region may be explored by a long-distance footpath, GR7. What is surprising is the sheer scale of that footpath. It starts at the coast close to Gibraltar, heading inland through two Natural Parks and the marvellous city of Ronda to reach a village at the edge of another Natural Park. Here the route divides. The northern branch heads north through more fine parks. The southern branch heads east, staying in, or close to, further parks as it skirts the southern edge of the Sierra Nevada, before turning north through a section of a National Park to reach the northern route. The combined early section of the walk covers almost 170 miles (270km), while each of the branches covers more than 275 miles (440km). If you combine the branches you will have completed 720 miles (1,150km) and climbed more than 88,500ft (27,000m), a major undertaking given that it must be accomplished in a much warmer climate than that experienced on any other long-distance walk in this book. But whether you complete this very fine route route in one

epic journey or over several visits, or even just complete a larger section, the rewards will be substantial.

Below, after the combined early section of the walk, the southern branch is considered in more detail; for the northern branch much briefer details are given.

The route starts in Tarifa, a fishing port with a fine old castle and buildings influenced by its Moorish heritage. Punta de Tarifa is the most southerly point of Continental Europe, just 10 miles (16km) from Africa, which is readily visible: ferries from the port cross the Straits of Gibraltar to and from Tangier. The narrowness of the Straits makes this a popular crossing point for migrating birds, and spring and autumn bring birdwatchers flocking to the area. Kite flyers and wind surfers also come, the winds in the Straits being both strong and (reasonably) dependable.

From the port GR7 heads west along the coast, and then turns north to reach Los Barrios, a delightful little town. The bull on the roundabout here is often taken to mark the start of the Route del Toro, the Bull Route that threads a way through a series of towns which see bullfighting as a proud heritage rather than the unpleasant cruelty that many non-Spaniards consider it. There are ranches in the area that rear bulls for the ring; there is a new ring in the town itself. A more agreeable attitude to wildlife was responsible for the setting up of the Parque Natural de Los Alcornocales, to the north of the town, which protects Spain's largest expanse of cork oaks. GR7 edges the southern limit of the park on its way to Los Barrios. From the town the route follows the park's eastern edge, staying close to a railway line before bearing off to reach the exquisite village of Castillo de Castellar, grouped around a castle that saw action in the conflict between Christians and Muslims. The village is a Spanish Historic/Artistic Monument and has been beautifully restored.

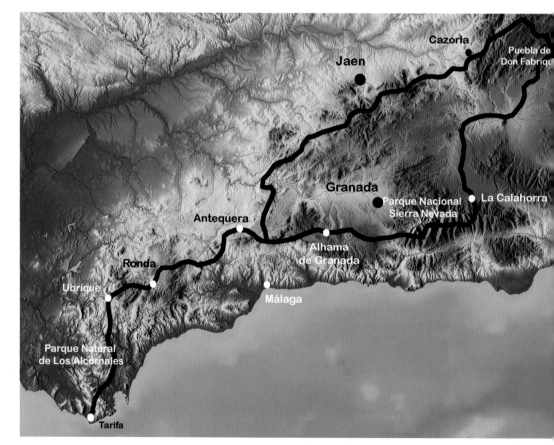

Cork oaks in the Parque Natural de Los Alcornales.

Beyond the village the route again follows the railway, offering a relief from route-finding, as in places GR7 is not well signed, to Jimena de la Frontera, another fine village. The castle here was built by the Moors on the site of a Roman fortress. To the west of the village, the Cueva de la Laja Alta has a strange collection of rock art. Much of the art is prehistoric, but several paintings of ships are probably from the Roman period. The juxtaposition of the two forms has baffled experts.

North of Jimena, GR7 crosses beautiful but remote farmland, with flower-rich meadows and copses, or larger woods, of cork oaks. Camping is inevitable on this section, as it is too far to walk from Jimena to Ubrique in one day, and there are no possibilities for accommodation that do not require a lengthy detour. The good news is that the area is quiet, and still within the Natural Park, so there is a good chance of studying the park's bird life at close quarters.

Ubrique, and the next village through which GR7 travels, Villaluenga del Rosario, are both official Pueblos Blancos, on Andalucía's 'central' village route. Ubrique is also a centre for leatherwork. From it the route heads west and after relatively flat sections finds itself among the hills of the Parque Natural Sierra de Grazalema. Though the hills are not high, barely topping 3,250ft (about 1,000m), some climbs are steep, the compensation being terrific views to limestone outcrops, before the route drops down into Montejaque, a centre for walking in the eastern end of the park. From here the route is poorly marked and occasionally scruffy on the short section to Ronda, which is arguably the most impressive town on the GR.

One of Spain's oldest towns, Ronda is built around the *tajo* (gorge) of the Guadalevín River, a 390ft (120m) gash that cuts the town in half. The older, more interesting section lies east of the nineteenth-century Puente Nuevo which crosses the deepest point. There is much to admire in the old town, including a house where the Spanish writer Cervantes once stayed and several excellent museums. In the newer section of the town, the bullring is claimed to be one of the oldest and finest in the world. The well-heeled walker can stay at the town's Parador (luxury hotel, usually in a fine old building), the only one on GR7.

From Ronda GR7 heads north (a tricky exit, signs being poor/non-existent) to Arriate, and then forges a route across remote, switchback country, with great views and the occasional fine, quiet village – Serrato, Ardales – set in country where olive and almond trees abound. Beyond Ardales there is superb walking through rugged country with expansive views towards huge reservoirs (built in the 1920s to provide both electricity and drinking water for Malaga) to the north, before the route reaches El Chorro. At the village the 2 mile (3km) long, 590ft (180m) deep Los Gaitanes Gorge is crossed by an unlikely-looking walkway, built originally to provide a means of getting materials to the site of the hydro-electric plant. It is known as the King's Way after Alfonso XIII braved the narrow, exposed path. The walkway fell into disrepair, and after several deaths it was closed. However, it is now being restored, so in future walkers may be able to follow it for close-up views of climbers on the gorge walls.

A steep climb is now needed to reach more fine country, before a descent into the amazingly steep village of Valle de Abdalajis. Ahead the route eases around the northern edge of the Parque Natural Torcal – well worth visiting for its natural sculptures – before reaching Antequera. The town, rivalling Ronda as the largest town on GR7, has an interesting older quarter grouped around the Moorish fortress of Alcabaza, reached through the Arco de los Gigantes, the Gate of the Giants. A short distance east of the town, at Villeneuva de Cauche, GR7 splits.

The southern section, a personal favourite, now heads east. It is largely unsigned, but follows good paths. That said, a guidebook and

Ronda is one of the highlights of GR7. Set on a hill above the valley of the Guadalevín River, the town is a delight with an array of fine buildings and a couple of interesting museums. But the most dramatic feature is El Tajo, the 120m deep gorge which bisects the town. The bridge which crosses the gorge (which at night is floodlit – ABOVE) is one of the most photographed spots in Andalucía. The photograph (LEFT) is of the old bridge at the base of the gorge. Beyond are the hills of the Serrania de Ronda, a collection of small *sierras*.

OPPOSITE
ABOVE Between Montejaque and Ronda, GR7 threads a way through the southern peaks of the Sierra de las Cumbres.
BELOW The landscape near Ronda.

map are essential for deciding which good path of several is correct. You soon reach Riogordo, a neat village with Moorish origins that was once the headquarters of bandits who used the folded local country to escape detection. Further on, the route uses the trackbed of an old railway, from which there are expansive views south down the Gárdenas valley and ahead to Cerro de los Torreones (3,178ft/969m). Beyond an old tunnel (torch not required), down left, is the village of Ventas de Zafarraya, named for an old inn which stood at the top of the long climb out of the valley; the village has expanded recently and may be a handy stopover.

You now enter the Parque Natural Sierras de Tejeda, Almijara y Alhama, following an old drove route through fine woodland to reach Alhama de Granada. Perched at the edge of a large gorge, the village has a long history linked to the thermal springs that give it its name (al-hamma means 'hot springs' in Arabic); the remains of Moorish fortifications can still be seen. GR7 follows the steep-sided gorge out

of town, continuing through cork oak woods and almond groves to Arenas del Rey, from where road and track lead you to an information centre for the park. The centre is in an old resin factory and has a fascinating display on the old craft of extracting resin from the local trees, which are a subspecies of maritime pine. The resin was once used to make pitch for waterproofing boats and roofs, and the factory distilled it to make turpentine.

Beyond Jayena, another Moorish village, a woodland track passes a magnificent viewpoint of the peaks of the Sierra de Almijara on the way to the Mesón Prados de Lopera, where there is always a throng of locals – walkers, cyclists, biker groups – suggesting (correctly) that it is a fine place to pause, and to eat and drink. From the restaurant, you are on the section of the route that passes closest to Granada, though for a glimpse of the city you will need to make a detour. Beyond the pretty villages of Albuñuelas and Restábal, you cross the motorway connecting the city to the south coast. GR7 continues through

ABOVE Antequera.
LEFT The Los Gaitanes Gorge at El Chorro.

OPPOSITE
LEFT The route into Riogordo follows a track through a country of cultivated fields interspersed with wild areas where cacti abound.
RIGHT Approaching Zafarraya, GR7 follows the trackbed of an old railway line, with views back towards Vilo, the highest peak of the Sierra de Alhama.

Nigüelas, another pleasant village, its main street tree-lined, to reach the Sierra Nevada National Park. Surprisingly, the mountain villages through which GR7 now travels, set on the southern hills of the National Park, are not on one of the 'official' Pueblos Blancos routes. They should be, for they are every bit as attractive.

The first is Lanjaron, too large perhaps to qualify as a village, and famous as a spa rather than a craft/agricultural village. There is an old Moorish castle whose watchtower was one of many across the landscape, all visually connected so that the defenders could pass on an early warning of an approaching Christian army. It is said that when Lanjaron was attacked in 1492 the commander of the castle, realizing that the town's capture was inevitable, threw himself to his death from the tower rather than suffer the ignominy of defeat.

From Lanjaron you walk through the Alpujarras, a series of lush valleys which carve into the high Sierras. These were the last stronghold of the Moors in Spain, a significant population living here until a failed uprising in 1568 led to their final expulsion. Within the area, you traverse a beautiful land of citrus, olive and almond groves, interspersed with crop fields, native trees, shrubs and flowers. There are also rugged open sections where there is an expansive view to the lower hills of the south – on clear days you can see Africa – and stunning little villages, none better in the western Alpujarras than Bubión. More fine walking, often through woodland, takes you to Trevélez, a charming place which was once the start point of ascents of Mulhacén, until the building of a road which takes walkers almost to the top has allowed a less arduous climb. Trevélez still attracts some walkers, and will be welcomed by carnivorous walkers as it is a centre for ham production, many of the restaurants being decorated with cured legs. Another speciality, here and in most other villages in the area, is a soup of chopped boiled egg and noodles. Served with hunks of fresh bread, this is excellent walking fare. The name varies, but is usually called *sopa piccadillo*, and that name will usually be understood.

There is a steep climb out of Trevélez, and then the route threads an exquisite path through fine woodland, pretty villages and occasional

LEFT The old railway trackbed towards Zafarraya. Just around the corner ahead there is a short but easily negotiated tunnel.

BELOW The gorge at Alhama de Granada. GR7 follows the path through the gorge, exiting close to El Ventorro, a delightful restaurant serving local dishes.

OPPOSITE
ABOVE Looking out over the Parque Natural de Tejeda, Almijara y Alhama from a viewpoint on the route south-east of Jayena.
BELOW Goat herd on the route in the Almijara section of the Natural Park.

open, rugged upland areas to reach Laroles. Here it turns north, losing the views south, across hillsides dotted with white villages. It now climbs through woodland to reach Puerto de la Ragua, the highest point on GR7 at an official height of 2,000m (6,560ft), which seems too exact to be accurate. The visitor complex here, which caters for summer walkers and cross-country skiers in winter, is a welcome stop before the downhill section to La Calahorra with its stupendous castle. The castle, very much in Italian style, was built by Christian Spain in the early nineteenth century on the site of the Moorish fortress. The somewhat austere exterior contrasts with the Renaissance interior, which includes a colonnaded courtyard. One owner was the illegitimate son of a cardinal who tried, but perhaps luckily failed, to marry Lucrezia Borgia.

From the castle it is possible to view the next part of the route, which crosses an arid, flat plain to reach the Parque Natural de la Sierra Baza, the low hills of which are the last upland section on GR7. Within the park the walk is mainly through farmland, with occasional sections of fine oak or pine forest, before you reach Baza, a larger town than the route has passed for many days. The excellent guidebook to GR7 suggests that the southern route now continues to Puebla de Don

Fadrique, but beyond Baza the countryside is very different from the high Sierras of the earlier route, and many will feel that Baza is a fitting end point if the continuation of the northern route is not to be contemplated. Indeed, a case could be made for finishing at La Calahorra, where the castle makes a stunning terminus.

BELOW Looking into the Trevélez valley and towards the high peaks of the Sierra Nevada invisible behind clouds.

OPPOSITE
ABOVE Looking back along the line of Pueblos Blancos on the southern slopes of the Sierra Nevada.
BELOW Pack horses are still regularly employed between the Pueblos Blancos as the roads are narrow, winding and slow.

THE NORTHERN ROUTE

There will be some who believe that the northern route is the better of the two options from Villenueva de Cauche, making the valid point that the compensation for not exploring the flank of the Sierra Nevada is a traverse of country that is off the beaten track, exploring a Spain that the tourist trade has, to date, largely ignored.

From Villenueva the route heads towards the mountains and the village of Villanueva del Rosario. From here you spend many delightful hours in olive groves and rich farmland, discovering that so few pass this way that the route is occasionally overgrown. You pass the vast Iznájar reservoir, the largest in Andalucía, and continue through the oak and pine forests of the Parque Natural Sierras Subbeticas to reach Priego de Córdoba, a pleasant town and a centre for olive oil production. More olive groves bring you to picturesque Alcalá la Real, where the remains of a nineteenth-century castle, built on much older Moorish foundations, perch above the town.

On the next section of the walk there are views ahead to the Sierra de Alta Coloma, and to the south the Sierra Nevada, as you pass through more woodland to reach the wilder country of the Alta Coloma, the route climbing above the 4,920ft (1,500m) contour before descending to Carchelejo. Easier walking follows, to the Parque Natural de la Sierra Mágina, where occasionally jagged peaks rise to almost 7,000ft (2,100m). GR7 climbs through the park, reaching the Puerto de la Mata pass at 5,412ft (1,650m), with great views, particularly to the Sierra Nevada; then it continues along the park's northern edge to Bedmar with its ruined castle.

Now it climbs steeply uphill before descending to Jódar, a local capital under the Moors. The next bit of walking is easier, but the country becomes wilder again when you reach the huge Parque Natural Sierras de Cazorla, Segura y Las Villas. GR7 threads its way through the vast forests of pines that make up much of the park, with occasional views to jagged rock faces. On the way you pass a number of *ermitas* (pilgrimage chapels) set among the crags. That of the Virgen de la Cabeza holds a very early image of the Virgin; this was brought to the area in the seventh century, but then hidden among the rocks, its position known only to a shepherd, when the Moors captured the area.

On again, and GR7 stays close to the Guadalaquivir River, offering a beautiful contrast of nearby river scenery and far views of the magnificent Cazorla Park. It then turns east, through a final, equally impressive, section of the park before traversing farmland to reach Puebla de Don Fadrique.

Calahorra castle. In the distance is the plain crossed to link the southern route with the northern.

Travel

By air It is possible to fly direct to Málaga, Almeriá and Granada, many budget airlines offering Málaga as a destination for travellers to the Costa del Sol. Trains from these cities reach Algeciras, close to Tarifa.

By rail Algeciras can also be reached from Madrid, which has connections from across Europe.

By road Andalucía is well served by motorways and good-quality major roads that connect to the rest of Spain. However, as elsewhere, the fastest roads only reach major population centres. Inland Andalucía has good roads, but these follow the contours of the mountains and so can be slow to travel on. On the southern flank of the Sierra Nevada the roads are tortuous and so can be both very slow and, occasionally, terrifying.

Maps and guides

Walking the GR7 in Andalucía, Kirstie Shirra and Michelle Lowe, Cicerone.

This guide is brilliant, the authors managing to pack the vast route into a single 285-page volume – a masterly achievement. The route description will ensure that you stay on route, but taking maps as well is essential, because even with such an excellent guide mistakes can occur, and it is possible to be very lost indeed just a few hundred metres off route.

The full list of 1:50,000 Servicio Geografico del Ejercito maps is given in the guide. Not surprisingly the list is very long (thirty-seven maps), and will not be repeated here.

Waymarking

The guide suggested above is essential, as waymarking on the route varies from the adequate to the non-existent. In principle the whole route is waymarked with the standard red and white GR marks, sometimes on rocks and trees, sometimes with specific signs. In practice there are many areas where the signing is poor or absent. Also helpful are the occasional information boards on GR7 and other walking routes. However, nothing is as useful as the guidebook.

Accommodation

The agricultural land through which, in general, the route travels has a large number of villages in almost all of which the walker will be able to find accommodation. This varies from quality hotels to more basic *pensións*, with much in between. There are a handful of sections where you will need to travel long distances between such places, and on these camping is essential. These sections tend to be in the wilder areas covered by the National Park and Nature Parks, and basic campsites are available within these. Wild camping within the parks should be avoided, particularly in summer when the risk of fire is high. Camping is forbidden in the Tejeda, Almijara y Alhama Park, and in the Baza Park between May and November.

Equipment

Most walkers choose early or late summer to avoid the hottest times. At those times shorts, a T-shirt and a hat (the latter essential for most walkers) will usually suffice, though it is always worth taking waterproofs because summer's heat can bring thunderstorms. Winter is cooler, of course, but then snow is likely on higher ground and accommodation and other facilities will be limited.

Climate

Being about as far south as it is possible to go in Europe, Andalucía is hot in the summer, with temperatures reaching beyond 104°F/40°C – not much fun for the walker. Spring and autumn are cooler, but also wetter.

Hazards

The chief hazard will be the heat and its attendant dehydration. The most dangerous natural hazard is one you are unlikely to see. Lataste's viper is about 2ft/60cm long, pale grey or brown with a darker zig

Though not poisonous, ladder snakes are extremely aggressive with an unpleasant bite. The specimen below, which was about 5ft (1.5m) long, was not pleased at all about being helped off the road and out of danger, responding to the assistance in a very unfriendly manner.

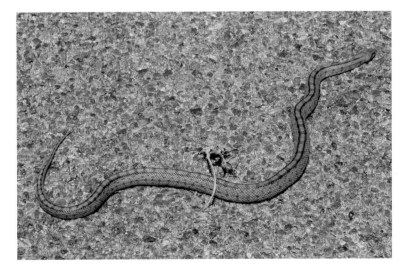

National Parks and Wildlife

One of the joys of GR7 is the number of parks through which it makes its way. Below, brief details of the flora and fauna of each are given.

Parque Natural de Los Alcornocales A 665 sq. mile (1,700 sq. km) park set up to protect the cork oaks that give the park its name (the name means 'cork oak groves'). Cork is a layer between the outer bark and the tree's living tissue, and has been collected for centuries; the harvesting of it, about every twelve years, does not endanger the tree if carried out with great care. Bird life includes the Spanish imperial eagle and the black-winged kite among 18 raptor species, 3 species of stork (white, black and the rare yellow-billed), golden oriole and hoopoe. Mammals include common genet, wildcat and the introduced Egyptian mongoose, as well as 20 species of bat.

Parque Natural Sierra de Grazalema This 203 sq. mile (520 sq. km) park was the first to be created in Andalucía, in 1984. The bird life includes a large colony of griffon vultures, Bonelli's eagle, rock bunting, rock thrush and black wheatear. Mammals include the rare Spanish ibex as well as 19 bat species. Reptiles include Lataste's viper and the horseshoe whip snake.

Parque Natural El Torcal A tiny park, just 5 sq. miles (12 sq. km), set up to protect an extraordinary karst landscape, with limestone tors carved by eons of rain and wind. The park flora includes more than 30 species of orchid, while the animal life includes Lataste's viper, Montpellier snake – one of Europe's largest snakes, adults reaching over 6ft (2m) – and the spiny-footed lizard.

Parque Natural Sierras de Tejeda, Almijara y Alhama A 156 sq. mile (400 sq. km) park named in part for the *tejo*, the yew tree, though there are now far fewer specimens than formerly, farmers having felled the trees because they are toxic to domestic animals. Birds include golden eagle, crag martin and blue rock thrush. The mammal most likely to be seen is the Spanish ibex, the park being a stronghold where the population has increased significantly in the last few years.

Parque Nacional Sierra Nevada A huge park extending to almost 350 sq. miles (900 sq. km), famous not only for its mountain scenery – in terms of peak height, the number of peaks of over 3,000m (about 9,850ft) makes the Sierra Nevada the second highest range in Europe after the Alps – but for its bird life, with over 60 species being resident, and butterflies, over 100 species having been identified. Mammals include the Spanish ibex and the beech marten.

Parque Natural de la Sierra Baza In this park covering 211 sq. miles (540 sq. km), crested and thekla larks are among about 100 bird species to have been recorded; 30 mammal species have also been identified, including common genet, wild boar and roe deer; and 17 species of reptiles and 8 amphibians also breed here.

Parque Natural Sierras Subbeticas The park covers 125 sq. miles (320 sq. km) of limestone plateau, varying in height from 1,650ft to 4,920ft (500m to 1,500m). Park flora includes two endemic forms: *Narcissus bugei*, a wild daffodil, and the beautiful mirror orchid. Bird life includes the peregrine falcon (the park's emblem), alpine swift and alpine accentor. Mammals include, unusually, the mouflon.

Parque Natural de la Sierra Mágina The name Sierra Mágina, given to the area by the Moors, means 'mountain of spirits'. Covering 78 sq. miles (200 sq. km) the limestone park is famous for its rich variety of plant life, including many orchids and aromatic plants. One very rare endemic is the red Cazorla violet, but there are several other unusual species, including the gromwell *Lithodora nitida*, and a subspecies of the rock rose. The park is also home to 20 orchid varieties. Mammal species include the pardel lynx, a beautifully marked cat that is now found only in a few isolated parts of Andalucía. The pardel is critically endangered, the population probably numbering no more than 200. Reptiles include Lataste's viper.

Parque Natural Sierras de Cazorla, Segura y Las Villas An enormous park, covering over 780 sq. miles (2,000 sq. km) of upland (the whole park area lies above 1,970ft/600m). Much of the area is forested, often with the laricio subspecies of black pine. It is claimed that some specimens of the pine are over 1,300 years old, though many experts believe that a figure of 500 years is probably closer to the mark; either way, these are ancient trees. Endemic plants include a subspecies of the blue columbine, which grows in just one small area. Over 180 birds have been recorded in the park, as well as over 50 mammals. Also recorded are over 100 butterflies, 12 amphibians and 21 reptiles, including the Spanish algyroides, a rather plain, brown lizard that is endemic.

TOP ABOVE Corn bunting.
ABOVE Thekla lark.

RIGHT
TOP Purple viper's bugloss.
CENTRE ABOVE Crown daisy.
CENTRE BELOW Red star-thistle and friends.
BELOW Iberian water frog.

OPPOSITE Iberian rock lizard.

The Cares Gorge

PICOS DE EUROPA, SPAIN

The Picos de Europa are a range of high limestone peaks separated from the main mass of the Cantabrian Mountains in north-eastern Spain. Somewhat neglected by walkers, the Picos offer spectacular scenery, with dramatic gorges, jagged peaks and picturesque valleys. This wonderful combination led to the creation of Spain's first National Park in 1918. The National Park was enlarged in 1995, and now covers most the three well-defined masses (Cornión, Los Urrieles and Andara) that form the Picos. The masses are separated by deep, narrow gorges carved out over the millennia by rivers heading north to the Bay of Biscay.

One of the rivers, the Cares, separates Cornión and Los Urrieles. Its gorge, the Garganta del Cares, is the most exquisite of all the gorges as well as having the advantage of being inaccessible except on foot. The

walk is, though, aided by a sensational walkway which was picked out of the sheer rock wall of the northern side of the gorge about a hundred years ago, as part of the construction of a hydro-electric system, which fed some of the river water to a power station at Poncebos by way of an aqueduct. The walkway allowed men to inspect the canal regularly: and they still do, which means that the path is inspected and maintained.

The gorge is about 6 miles (10km) long between the villages of Puente Poncebos and Cain, but most walkers make an out-and-back walk from one or other, as it is a very long way between the villages by road and, unless there are two cars, expensive to organize. You can

Goatherders at the start of the gorge walk.

start at either village, of course, but beginning at Poncebos has the advantage of starting with the only climb (and therefore finishing with a descent).

From the road end at Puente Poncebos a track zigzags upwards, but a good alternative is to follow the wide donkey trail closer to the river, saving the climb until your muscles have warmed up. Soon the path enters the gorge, where stupendous walls of rock, shimmering white in the sun, rise from the narrow belt of vegetation that hugs the river. Ultimately a long climb leads up an unstable scree slope to reach the upper path. This path is awesome (and only partly protected by handrails), mainly because, unlike Sentier Martel in the Verdon Gorge (see page 88) where the route is close to the base of the gorge, it perches halfway up the rock face so that there are views down as well as up. There is also a view of the aqueduct that winds in and out of the rock walls, occasionally disappearing for long distances. Look out for climbers at work on the sheer faces. On my last visit the climbers were apparently being watched by a flock of nine Griffon vultures, who seemed rather too interested in their progress.

On the path you progress by way of a short damp tunnel, and then through a section of gorge so narrow that the sun is largely excluded. Later, waterfalls cascade down the gorge walls; the splashed rock is a paradise for mosses and lichen, while above crag martins wheel in the sky. The path crosses and then recrosses the gorge, before entering a longer, damper tunnel. Beyond, you cross a delightful alpine meadow – look out for Cleopatra butterflies here – to reach Cain and a collection of reasonable stops for food and drink. Now all that remains is to enjoy it all again on the way back.

Walk information

Map: Adrados Ediciones 1:25,000 Picos de Europa Macizos Central y Oriental (Los Urrieles y Andara). Start/finish: Puente Poncebos. Length: 12½ miles (20km). Ascent: 850ft (260m).

BELOW Griffon vulture.

The Haute Randonnée Pyrénéenne

FRANCE AND SPAIN

According to Greek mythology, it was Heracles – or Hercules, to give the Greek hero his Roman name – who created the Pyrénées. When he visited the Spanish king, Bebrycius, during the tenth of his twelve labours (the one requiring him to kill the monster Geryon) Heracles became the lover, or perhaps the rapist, of the king's daughter, Pyrene. She gave birth to a snake and fled in terror to an isolated wilderness, where she died. Heracles followed her and, finding her body, buried her beneath a pile of rocks. So great was the cairn he erected that it formed a mountain range between Spain and France and the range was named for the dead princess. In Spanish the mountains are the Pirineos, in Catalan the Pireneus, but the common name for them is the French form, Pyrénées.

The true history of the creation of the Pyrénées is more prosaic, though no less interesting. The mountains are older than the Alps, uplifted during the process of mountain folding known as the Variscan or Hercynian orogeny about 280 million years ago. Later the folded rock that was the basis of the Pyrénées was submerged. The sediments that were laid down formed limestones that were then raised, folded and heated as Spain was forced towards France. That final folding, about 150 million years ago, and subsequent erosion formed the peaks we see today.

Contrary to the general view, the Pyrénées are not a single chain of peaks: rather they comprise two distinct ranges, each about 125 miles (200km) long, which overlap for only a little more than 6 miles (10km) where the River Garonne flows across the border from Spain into France. Even the view of two ranges can be challenged, for the Pyrénées are complex, with occasional separated and overlapping ridges, particularly at the western end. The western chain is the higher of the two main ranges, rising several times above 3,000m (about 9,850ft) and reaching its highest point at the Pico d'Aneto (11,168ft/3,404m) on the Spanish side of the border. The three highest peaks of the Pyrénées lie in Spain, and the fourth highest, Vignemale (10,791ft/3298m), on the national border.

In the western Pyrénées erosion-resistant granites are flanked and overlain by limestones, as the peaks rise from the sharp south-eastern corner of the Bay of Biscay. They rise gradually, the first of the highest peaks appearing some 100 miles (160km) from the coast. From there, at a point south-west of Cauterets in France, the Pyrénées represent arguably the finest accessible mountain range in Europe. The Alps might be higher, but for the average walker they are often hazardous and therefore off limits. In contrast, the walker can penetrate the Pyrénées deeply, and will revel in the sharp limestone peaks and curious geological features. But caution is necessary: though rarely glaciated, the mountains are still high enough to provide a serious mountain environment, especially in poor weather – and the Pyrénées are renowned for summer snowstorms, when treacherous conditions are made worse by reduced visibility and cold.

To the east of the high peaks the fall in height of the Pyrénéan tops is even more gradual than the rise. Most experts claim that the high peaks end at Andorra, and the principality does indeed represent the last of the truly wild, rugged country. But east of Andorra there is still much of interest. There the peaks form a single and fascinating ridge, which includes the Pic du Canigou (9,132ft/2,784m), sacred to the Catalans. East again, the Pyrénées fall towards the Mediterranean. Here Hannibal crossed the Col du Perthus on his way to Rome, while at the nearby Col de Panissors the Romans raised a 'trophy' to celebrate the conquest of Gaul. Finally, at Cap Cerbère, named for the three-headed dog that guarded the entrance to the Underworld in Greek mythology, the Pyrénées reach the sea.

There are few of the big lakes that often characterize mountain areas, and few low passes. Ice Age glaciation has carved a succession of magnificent cirques (closed valleys that end with a semicircle of usually steep cliffs). Winter snows give rise to streams (*gaves*), which tumble over the cliffs to form huge waterfalls; that in the Cirque de Gavarnie has a total fall of 1,387ft (423m), the highest in Europe. Gavarnie and the nearby Cirque de Troumouse form the centrepiece of a French

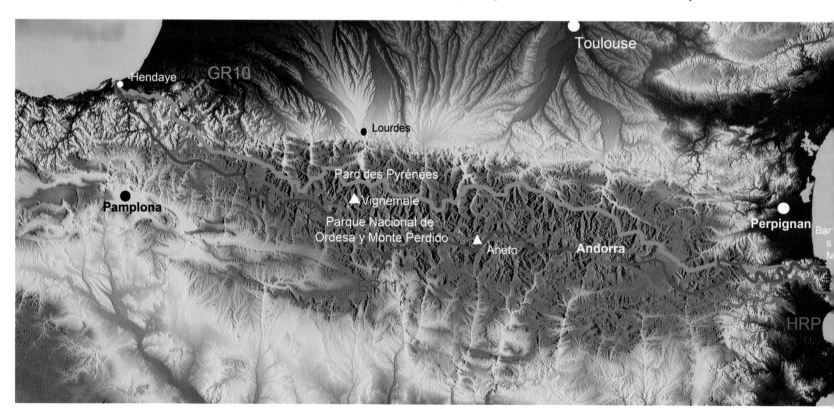

RIGHT Medieval manuscript illustration of the battle at the Col de Roncevaux. At the col there is a monument to Roland (said to stand where he was buried) and a small chapel.

BELOW Campsite in the central Pyrénées.

National Park, contiguous with the Parque Nacional de Ordesa y Monte Perdido in Spain. Within the Ordesa park lies the ice cave of Grotte Casteret. Discovered in 1926 by the French speleologist Norbert Casteret, this is one of the most extraordinary of all Pyrénéan geographical features, its microclimate maintaining ice even during the summer.

The streams and falls of the northern flank of the Pyrénées are an indication of the climatic divide formed by the range. Abundant rain falls on the eastern (French) side, while the west (Spanish) is relatively arid. The range is also a cultural divide, a formidable 250 mile (400km) land barrier which historically could be crossed at only a few passes that lay below 2,000m (6,560ft). Many claim the mountains are the most significant cultural divide in Europe, separating the Iberian Peninsula, with its close ties to Africa, from the rest of the Continent. They point to the slower development of a hot, dry Iberia relative to France with its connections to Britain, Germany and Italy. But though this is undeniable, it ignores the role of Spain and Portugal in spreading Western civilization across the world and disregards the existence of ancient trans-Pyrenean kingdoms such as Catalonia and Navarre, as well as that of the Romans.

The beauty and accessibility of the Pyrénées have resulted in the development of three outstanding long-distance walks. GR10 follows the base of the mountains on the French side, venturing to higher ground rarely and only occasionally touching the French–Spanish border. On the Spanish side, GR11 follows a similar logic. The Haute Randonnée Pyrénéenne, a high-level route known everywhere simply as the HRP, is more adventurous, seeking out the higher ground and occasionally crossing from France to Spain and back again.

Each walk is demanding. GR10 covers 560 miles (900km) and involves almost 165,000ft (50,000m) of ascent and descent. GR11 is 525 miles (840km), with about 131,000ft (40,000m) of ascent and descent. The HRP is shorter than either, but involves more ascent and descent, and occasionally crosses very difficult terrain – snow, ice and steep sections of rock where progress is aided by ladders and wires. GR10 crosses a wonderful array of scenery, varying from woodland to typical Mediterranean garrigue, from mountain to pasture. GR11 passes through much the same country, but is less wooded, the landscape more arid. The lack of tree shading means GR11 is often more arduous, as walkers must spend hours in the full glare of the sun. But they visit both landscapes on the HRP, as well as enjoying close-up views of some of Europe's most rugged mountainscapes.

The route description here concentrates on the HRP, noting where the route crosses the lower-level routes. Brief details of GR10 and GR11 are given later.

Pic du Midi d'Ossau and the Refuge de Pombie.

The HRP shares a start point with GR10, the Casino at Hendaye-Plage. Hendaye, set at the mouth of the Bidassoa, is the most south-westerly town in France, its beaches one of the more popular local tourist destinations.

The town was the birthplace of Martin Guerre, famous for his disappearance and replacement by an imposter who was accepted by Guerre's wife (though she was not necessarily entirely taken in) and lived with her for several years, fathering two children. The imposter was then unmasked and hanged for adultery and fraud, the real Martin Guerre having finally turned up. The saga is now probably more famous as the basis of the film *Sommersby*, starring Jodie Foster and Richard Gere, which romanticized the tale and transferred it from nineteenth-century France to post-Civil War America. In Hendaye's main square the Great Cross is carved with a curious array of alchemical symbols which have been 'translated' as predicting global catastrophe. The town's railway station is an important junction, as Spanish railway lines have a different gauge to those of the rest of Europe. In the station, in 1940, Adolf Hitler met Generalissimo Franco in a failed attempt to persuade him to enter the war on the Axis side.

The first section of the HRP follows GR10 to the Col d'Ibardin but then leaves it, the GR staying in France while the high route heads south-east into Spain and towards its first peak, the 2,950ft (900m) La Rhune. There is no need (unless you are a dedicated peak-bagger) to go to the summit, which stands on the national border, before you

descend to the Collado de Lizuniaga (*collado* is the Spanish form of the French *col*), where you meet GR11 and follow it along the national border and over a series of low *collados* in Spain to Collado Bagacheta, where the two part company. All three routes are now deep in Basque country. The origins of the Basques are disputed, though everyone agrees that they, and their language, are among the most ancient in Europe: walkers will soon become familiar with the typical white houses with coloured shutters, and place names rich in the letters 'k' and 'x'.

Beyond Arizkun, an attractive village famous for its carnivals, the HRP crosses undulating Basque farmland with patches of woodland to reach the Col de Roncevaux (Puerto de Ibañeta), where it rejoins GR11. At the col there is a monument to Roland, legendary hero of Charlemagne's army when, in 778, it marched into Spain to attack the cities of Pamplona and Zaragoza, which had been under Arab control since the Moorish invasions of the early eighth century. The invasion was indecisive: Charlemagne was forced to retreat without gaining a significant victory, though with some plunder. During the retreat, local Basques attacked the army, inconveniencing them rather than inflicting serious damage but forcing Charlemagne to dispatch men under Roland, a Breton captain, to act as a rearguard. On 15 August, a large

Campsite below the north face of Vignemale.

On the way from Porte de Boucharo to the Refuge des Sarradets and the Brèche de Roland.

Basque armies. The later battle established an independent Basque homeland, and echoes of it still underpin the recent problems between Basque separatists and the Spanish government.

The HRP now follows GR11, but soon leaves it to reach the French–Spanish border close to the Col d'Arnostéguy, below Urculu (3,900ft/1,149m), the summit of which is topped by the base of a Roman tower. It continues along the border ridge (and sections of GR10), with occasional detours to superb, lowerlying country with lush green or, sometimes, forested hillsides and valleys: the scenery is idyllic, though the route marking leaves much to be desired and you are likely to put your map and compass to use before you reach Larrau, a small but pretty and well-appointed village.

Near by is the Col d'Orgambideska, a famous lookout for bird-watchers. Many of the Pyrénéan passes are used each autumn by hunters, who shoot migrating birds. The shooting rights are auctioned every three years and, to the hunters' anger, in 1979 bird lovers bought the rights for this col and banned hunting. Orgambideska is now one of the most important places on the range to watch birds, particularly raptors – black and red kites, honey buzzards and marsh harriers – but also black storks, cranes and more common species.

The col is a detour or variant of the HRP, which now climbs the Pic d'Orhy on the French–Spanish border, at 6,616ft (2,017m) the first 2,000m peak you reach. The route then follows the border ridge south-east with a view south across the northern section of the Irati Forest, a huge expanse of beech and fir which includes several nature reserves. Among the almost 49,400 acres (20,000ha) of trees you can find black and white-backed woodpeckers and many other species. Animals include wild boar, roe and red deer, and red squirrels.

force, it is unclear who, attacked the rearguard, killing Roland and many men. The battle became the subject of the earliest French epic poem, the eleventh-century *Chanson de Roland* (Song of Roland), the basis of Roland's legend. By the time the poem was written, a relatively minor battle between two groups of Christians had become a fight between a Christian army and a vast Muslim horde (the latter occasionally said to have numbered 400,000). Beside the monument, said to stand where Roland was buried, there is a small chapel.

The col, a handy crossing between France and Spain, was later the site of two further battles, in 811 and 824, between Frankish and

Leaving the ridge the HRP reaches the Refuge de Belagua (also called the Refuge Angel Oloron) in Spain. Acessible from a cross-border road the refuge is often busy, but it can usually offer accommodation as well as meals and drinks. Some of the traffic using the road here will be heading for Arette-la-Pierre-St-Martin, just across the border. In winter this is a thriving winter sports centre, and at all times it attracts cavers from around the world. At over 50 miles (80km) in length and 4,500ft (1,400m) deep the Gouffre de la Pierre-St-Martin is one of the deepest and most extensive cave systems in the world. An alternative route for the HRP – recommended if the

ABOVE The Brèche de Roland. The path from the Refuge des Sarradets to the gap can be seen crossing the snow slope to the left of the walker.
LEFT The Brèche can be reached from both the French and Spanish sides. The photograph shows the cliffs on the French side.

weather is poor as the next stage, though reasonably obvious in good visibility, is not easy to follow otherwise and passes through rugged country – goes via Arette, and then follows GR10 to Lescun.

The main route to Lescun forges a way through beautiful limestone country, the rock fluted by water and the passage of time, south of the Pic d'Anie (8,213ft/2,504m). GR10 and the HRP leave the village southward together, but GR10 soon heads east, while the HRP continues south, reaching the boundary of France's Parc National des Pyrénées at Pont d'Itchaxe.

The Cirque de Gavarnie.

This section of the HRP through the park is one of the highlights of the walk. The route is dominated by the Pic du Midi d'Ossau (9,460ft/2,884m) which, despite its formidable appearance, was first climbed in the nineteenth century (a claimed ascent 200 years earlier has now been discounted). Your next objective is Vignemale. Geologically this peak is curious, with a base of limestone and a top third of flysch, a sedimentary rock formed from the rapid deposition of sandstone and clay on the ocean bottom, Vignemale having been thrust up by tectonic activity aeons ago. The north face has several difficult and serious rock climbs, but you can reach the summit by a relatively straightforward route – though as it follows the edge of the Glacier d'Ossoue you will need ice-climbing equipment (rope, crampons, ice axe), even if a trench-like path carved by the feet of the

many who have preceded you is evident, as there may be hidden crevasses. The ascent passes several caves carved by the eccentric Franco-Irish Count Henry Russell-Killough, who climbed the peak thirty-three times in the late nineteenth/early twentieth centuries and sheltered in the caves with his guides. There is a statue to the count in Gavarnie, to which the HRP now heads.

The best route leads south to the Porte de Boucharo (7,511ft/2,290m), and then climbs to the Refuge des Sarradets below the Brèche de Roland. In the Song of Roland, the mythical hero survives the battle at Roncevaux but is defeated. Anxious to prevent his magic sword, Durandal, from being captured, Roland smashes it into the cliffs, cutting the famous gap named for him; but he fails to destroy the sword, which he then throws into a stream. From the

refuge, the climb to the Brèche is usually straightforward, as a safe route is carved in the snow slope early in the season.

From Sarradets, the HRP follows the path eastwards, and then descends the steep Échelle des Sarradets to the base of the Cirque de Gavarnie, bearing left to reach the village. Gavarnie, a stop on the pilgrims' route to Santiago de Compostela, is disappointing: the magnificent cirque – Victor Hugo called it 'Nature's Coliseum' – attracts crowds of visitors, and much of the village is given over to catering for them, not always in fine style.

The HRP leaves Gavarnie along the track to the cirque and then climbs steadily to the Hourquette d'Alans (7,970ft/2,430m) before descending to Lac des Gloriettes and following the D176 to Héas. This is great country, but I prefer to take a variant of a more direct route

from Gavarnie, through the Bois de Coumely. The time saved allows a visit to the Cirque de Troumouse, not as grand as Gavarnie's, but still superb and with the advantage that you are likely to be alone with the view. The walk from Héas is unrelenting: a 3,600ft (1,100m) climb to Horquette de Héas (8,554ft/2,608m) – during which you exit the National Park – continuing to the national border at Porte de Barroude before a descent of over 4,500ft (1,400m) to Parzán in Spain, where the HRP joins GR11.

The two routes head east, with fine views south to the Punta Suelza (8,888ft/2,972m) and the Pico de Posets (at 11,070ft/3,375m the second highest peak in the Pyrénées) to reach the Refuge de Viados. Here GR11 turns east and the HRP heads north into France over the Porte d'Aygues Tortes (8,800ft/2,683m), another high and poorly marked pass. It then traverses further magnificent mountain country, enhanced by a succession of fine lakes. But beware: the going is hard, with steep scree, boulder fields and remnant snow making life difficult. From the Lac du Portillon, formed in 1929 to feed a hydro-electric power station, the walk gets tougher still, being largely unmarked and including the highest pass on the walk (Col Inférieur de Literole, at 9,784ft/2,983m), from which the descent (into Spain) is very steep and often icy well into the summer.

The HRP reaches the Refuge de la Renclusa (the usual starting point for an ascent of Pico de Aneto) and then crosses more superb, but uncompromising, country to rejoin GR11 close to Estany de Mar, a beautifully sited lake, and the Parque National d'Aigüestortes i Estany de Sant Maurici. GR11 heads deep into the park, while the HRP turns north, using duckboards occasionally to aid progress through boggy forest, and then a section of road to reach Salardu, a village with a fine old centre and a thirteenth-century church with an octagonal tower. From the village there is another remote and poorly signed section of the route. This climbs the Tuc de Marimanya (8,731ft/2,662m), which offers expansive views, and continues through remote, poorly signed mountainscapes to reach the Refuge Enric Pujol, an aluminium, prefabricated hut that many a walker struggling to keep on the route has welcomed.

The next stage of the HRP is through country that is as wild and impressive as any previous stage. It is poorly signed, but as it is lower and easier to negotiate, you can enjoy the landscape without the pressure of altitude and weather worries. That the country is relatively

The Cirque de Troumouse.

inaccessible to all except the committed walker, and has fewer big, named peaks to act as a magnet, means that walkers are likely to be alone with their thoughts. Eventually the route heads for France, reaching the national border after a steep climb to the Porte de Boet (8,266ft/2,520m).

But the stay in France is short, just two or three hours, before you enter Andorra, an independent principality which thrives on a mix of tourism and high finance, and the third country traversed by the HRP. The HRP crosses the mountains of northern Andorra to reach the Valle d'Incles, which runs down to Soldeu, a winter sports centre, before returning to France close to l'Hospitalet-près-l'Andorre, on the main route from France to the principality. Legend has it that the 'hospital' (travellers' refuge) of the village's name was founded in the early eleventh century when a chevalier was caught in an unexpected snowstorm near the Col de Puymorens. The imperilled knight killed his horse, sliced it open and crawled inside, vowing that if he survived the ordeal he would endow a refuge. He did survive, and built not only the first refuge but an oratory, which still exists. The Col de Puymorens, a pass intimately connected with the Tour de France, lies to the south of the village.

LEFT Mist forming on the east side of the ridge at the Porteille de Siscaro where the HRP moves back into France from Andorra.

BELOW Looking east from near the Col des Gourgs Blancs to Lac des Iselots and Lac de Couillaouas.

LEFT The solar furnace at Odeillo, near Font Romeu.
BELOW LEFT The Abbey of St-Martin-du-Canigou.
BELOW RIGHT The summit of Pic du Canigou.

The spooky woodland below the Pic de Sailfort.

Puymorens is now bypassed by a tunnel that leads directly to the village, and the HRP bypasses it too, heading north-east steeply, and then east more gently to join GR10. The GR offers an alternative route east for those not wishing to tackle Pic Carlit, the dauntingly steep peak that rises to the south-east. Both routes cross the Col de Coume d'Agnel (8,102ft/2,470m) to reach the northern shore of the Étang de Lanoux. There GR10 heads east along the Grave valley to gain the western shore of the Lac des Bouillouses, while the HRP tackles Pic Carlit head on, taking a route that requires scrambling to reach the 9,580ft (2,921m) summit. As the highest peak in the eastern Pyrénées, the top is a marvellous viewpoint. But enjoyment of the view and the satisfaction of reaching the top are tempered by the need to make the descent, for which you need both to scramble and to negotiate steep scree.

The HRP and GR10 now follow the same route, descending the valley of La Têt River and then crossing roads east of the Font Romeu, another winter sports centre and home to an altitude-training facility for athletes. At nearby Odeillo is the world's most powerful solar furnace. Using almost 10,000 mirrors to concentrate energy from the sun, the furnace can reach temperatures exceeding 5400°F/3000°C.

At the Col de la Perche (5,179ft/1,579m) the two routes part company. GR10 heads east while the HRP continues south to Eyne and the Eyne Nature Reserve, an area of wooded valleys and alpine meadows established primarily to protect bird species including capercaillie, honey buzzard, red-backed shrike and rock thrush. The walk through this delightful reserve ends with a climb to the Col d'Eina (9,079ft/2,786m) on the French–Spanish border.

Walking along the border you reach GR11 at the Col (Collado) de Noucreus (9,181ft/2,799m). The HRP and GR11 continue along the ridge to the Col de Tirapitz (9,122ft/2,781m), and then descend into Spain. GR11 then turns south, staying in Spain, while the HRP heads back to France, climbing to the border at Porte de Mourens (7,816ft/2,383m). The route then stays high and in France as it crosses wide plateaux – the view ahead dominated by the Pic de Canigou, the last high peak of the Pyrénées – before descending to rejoin GR10 at the Refuge de Marialles.

The HRP and GR10 both head towards Canigou, but while the GR crosses the peak's northern flank, the HRP climbs steadily – and, in the final section, steeply with some scrambling required – to the summit (9,132ft/2,784m). Because of the peak's isolated position, which means that it dominates the area, for many years it was assumed that it was the highest Pyrénean peak. To the Catalans Canigou was a sacred mountain. In 1009 a monastery was built below it, at St Martin-de-Canigou, endowed by Guifred, Count of Cerdanya, as a way of atoning for his murder of his son. The Benedictine house became famous as a place of pilgrimage and sanctity. Then, in 1276, Pedro III of Aragon claimed to have climbed it and found, at the summit, a lake from which a fire-breathing dragon rose – a find that did much to raise Canigou's profile in the Catalan consciousness. The peak remains a special place for Catalans and has been the subject of many songs and poems.

An easy path descends the northern flank of Canigou and rejoins GR10. Here you turn east along a very pleasant, mainly downhill, wooded path to reach the Auberge de Batère. From this the GR heads towards Arles-sur-Tech, while the HRP stays a little to the north, following easy tracks to Amélie-les-Bains, a village with an interesting, tight, cobbled old centre. The local hot, sulphur-rich springs were exploited by the Romans and are now used to alleviate the symptoms of rheumatism.

By now you have descended 8,200ft (2,500m) from the summit of Canigou; Amélie lies at just 820ft (250m). But there are still hills to cross before you descend the last metres to the sea. The next stage of the HRP involves a long climb to the top of the Roc de France (4,756ft/1,450m), where the HRP rejoins GR10. The high route now follows the national border briefly before making one last foray into Spain and then crossing back into France for the last time. It climbs through spooky woodland, staying close to the national border all the way to the Pic de Sailfort (2,922ft/891m), from which the views to the Côte Vermeille are superb. At the peak the border turns south, but the HRP and GR10 continue east with little further difficulty, descending for the last time to reach Banyuls-sur-Mer, once a village that thrived on smuggling goods to and from Spain but now a tourist centre for those seeking sun and fine wines. Here you should make your way to the beach, remove your boots and paddle in the warm Mediterranean. You have earned it.

Looking down on Aset, on GR10.

GR10

In its western section GR10 crosses similar country to that of the HRP, mostly on lower slopes, though early on there is a section of ridge walking along the national border which involves several significant climbs. There are also significant climbs, totalling over 5,900ft (1,800m), on the day from Estérençuby, a delightful village set in a lovely valley to the east of St-Jean Pied-de-Port, to the Col Bagargiak. Further east, beyond Lescun, the route includes a section of the Chemin de la Mâture. This path, literally the 'Mast Road', was cut into the sheer face of the valley of the River Aspe close to Etsaut to allow easy transport of timber that was to be used in the construction of ships for the French navy. The road was 1,500 yards (1,200m) long and up to 650ft (200m) above the river. Not all of it is now accessible, but what is offers a sensational walk, though not one for the faint-hearted. While on the path, imagine what is must have been like to be the driver of the horse-drawn cart loaded with tree trunks.

Further east, you can take variants of the 'standard' route for a close approach to Vignemale or to visit the Cirque de Gavarnie, though the GR does cross some excellent lower country. East again, GR10 stays on the French side of the mountains while the HRP is mostly in Spain, before the two routes link up to cover much of the western end of the range.

RIGHT The Chemin de la Mâture.

BELOW A short distance from Candanchù, a variant of GR11 passes close to Canfranc station where the old railway line from France to Spain exits the tunnel under the Col du Sombort. The eerie, now derelict station and railway carriages are a must for railway enthusiasts.

GR11

The Spanish GR has a more impressive start than either of its companion routes, beginning at the lighthouse at Cabo Higuer, a headland that pokes out into the Atlantic across the river mouth from Hendaye. As with GR10, the route starts gently, traversing farmland and wooded valleys, but soon joins the HRP on more mountainous terrain. Beyond, though the two routes touch occasionally, GR11 crosses the foothills rather than the high tops, and spends longer within the Irati Nature Reserve. East of Candanchù, GR11 offers an exceptional view of the Pic du Midi d'Ossau across the Ibón d'Anayet, and then a fine view of Vignemale before reaching the Parque Nacional de Ordesa y Monte Perdido. Within the park, the Brèche de Roland can be reached from the southern side, offering the chance of a long day's excursion, crossing the Brèche to visit the Cirque de Gavarnie. East of the park GR11 and the HRP link again, though often the GR takes an easier, lower line. It also penetrates deeper into the Parque National d'Aigüestortes i Estany de Sant Maurici. The route traverses southern Andorra, and then links up with the HRP one last time before ending as it began, at a lighthouse – this time that at Cabo de Creus. Here there is no beach offering a paddle for tired feet, but there is a stone seat for quiet contemplation.

OPPOSITE The Chemin de la Mâture.

BELOW The Parque Nacional de Ordesa y Monte Perdido.

Travel

By air It is possible to fly to Barcelona, Biarritz, Carcassone, Gerona, Pau, Perpignan and Toulouse. It is also possible to reach Pamplona and San Sebastián by air, but at present only by flying to Madrid and taking an internal flight.

By rail Hendaye and Banyuls-sur-Mer have train stations, as does Irún just across the border from Hendaye. Unless you are being dropped off and collected, both ends of GR11 require out-and-back walking to the places with public transport. At the western end, Irún is the closest readily accessible point. At the eastern end, the easiest option is to walk to Cadaqués, from where there is an irregular bus service to Figueras, which has a rail link to France, Gerona and Barcelona.

By road There is easy road access to each end of the walks, and to many points along the way.

Maps and guides

Pyrenean Haute Route, Ton Joosten, Cicerone.
The GR10 Trail, Paul Lucia, Cicerone.
Through the Spanish Pyrenees: GR11, a Long-distance Footpath, Paul Lucia, Cicerone.

These guides, and the maps below, are essential.

HRP: IGN 1:50,000 Carte de Randonnée nos. 1, 2, 3, 7, 8, 10 and 11, Editorial Alpina 1:40,000 Alduides Baztan, and Mapa Excursionista/Carte de Randonnée nos. 20, 22, 23 and 24.

GR10: IGN 1:50,000 Carte de Randonnée nos. 1–8, 10 and 11.

GR11: the very best option is GR11 Senda Pirenaica, a complete set of 1:40,000 maps for the whole route published by Edita Prames (ISBN 84 8321 062 2).

Waymarking

Both GR10 and GR11 are marked with the standard GR red and white stripes. A red and white cross means wrong direction. There are also signposts marked with the GR number. The only real difficulties with the routes are at the western end, where a plethora of tracks have been carved across farmland, giving rise to occasional confusion about which is the correct route. The guidebooks are extremely useful here, as are map and compass. The HRP is not waymarked along its length, though there are often standard red and white stripes, as well as paint daubs in other colours, and cairns. Occasionally there are no waymarks and the walker is left to forge a route using a guide, map, compass, perhaps a GPS system and a great deal of mountain craft.

Accommodation

By planning very carefully it is possible to complete all three routes using mountain refuges – numerous throughout the Pyrénées – and the French *gîtes d'étape* (not to be confused with the Gîtes de France system). There is no similar accommodation in Spain, but there are occasional mountain bothies on the Spanish side which can be used. However, planning does not account for the weather, or the possibility

that route finding, particularly on the HRP, might cause delays. A tent, cooking equipment, etc. are therefore essential. If a mountain refuge is full, there is usually an allocated camping ground near by which you can use, eating in the refuge.

In general, tents can be pitched anywhere, and having a tent certainly allows you to choose daily itineraries as the mood takes you. However, there are restrictions on camping within the National Parks. In France, the pitching of a small tent for one night between the hours of 19.00 and 09.00 is allowed, provided the site is more than one hour's walk from a metalled road. In Spain, in principle, camping is not allowed, but campers who pitch for a single night at altitude (above about 6,500ft/2,000m) in remote sites are unlikely to be bothered. Be discreet, pitching only as night falls and breaking camp in the early morning: leaving a tent pitched all day is inviting trouble and will likely spoil things for other walkers.

Equipment

This depends largely on when you travel and which route you follow. On GR10 or GR11 in summer, lightweight equipment including a sleeping bag and good storm gear will suffice. On the HRP ice axes and crampons will also be required, as will a good tent and a three-season sleeping bag. Don't forget your passport.

Climate

Lying to the south of the French Riviera, it is no surprise that the Pyrénées are warm, often hot, in summer. Temperatures of 86°F/30°C and more are not uncommon, but like all mountains, the peaks occasionally manufacture their own weather and summer's heat may be tempered by wind and rain, and even, on the higher ground, snow. To the west, the Atlantic blankets the peaks with moist air that brings more rain and mist. To the east the drier, hotter air from Africa offers a more stable summer, with hot, cloudless days being the norm. In winter both areas see snow, which walkers in early summer may find still lying on high ground.

Hazards

In summer the chief hazard will be the heat and its attendant dehydration. Ironically, in view of water being the best drink, the tourist agencies on both sides of the border warn against the possibility of contracting giardia from stream water polluted by infected Pyrénéan sheep. Giardia is an intestinal parasite that causes severe stomach pain, vomiting and evil-smelling diarrhoea. These symptoms can go away, only to reappear after a few days. Medical treatment will effect a cure, but on the grounds that prevention is better, get hold of a pump-action water purifier, as the filtration systems employed by such devices are better against parasitic cysts than iodine-based tablets.

Both the common adder and the more potent asp viper occur in the Pyrénées, each having been found to 8,200ft (2,500m).

National Parks and Wildlife

The French Parc National des Pyrénées, established in 1967, is the smallest of the five French mainland parks with an area of 178 sq. miles (457 sq. km). The park is long (about 50 miles/80km west to east) and, as might be expected, narrow (rarely more than 6 miles/10km and usually less). The southern boundary of the park is the border between France and Spain, and near Gavarnie the park is contiguous with Spain's Parque Nacional de Ordesa y Monte Perdido.

Over a hundred species of mammal are found within the park (about 70 per cent of the total number of French mammals). These include brown bear, genet, lynx, Pyrénéan chamois and Pyrénéan desman. The status of the bear is unclear. Although the species has widespread public support, local farmers are antagonistic and illegal shooting has driven the population to the edge of extinction: there are probably no more than a handful of animals left. There are probably more lynx, but the continued survival of the species is also threatened. Numbers of the cat-like genet are higher. In part, the creation of the park was to aid the survival of the Pyrénéan chamois (or isard), which had been overhunted. With protection the population has risen to over six thousand. The desman is unique to the Pyrénées. A relative of the shrew, and shrew-like in appearance, it is aquatic, favouring fast-flowing mountain streams to altitudes of about 4,000ft (1,200m). Never numerous, the desman is classified as vulnerable.

The mammal the walker is most likely to encounter is the alpine marmot. Despite the apparently perfect habitat the area offers, the animal had not been a Pyrénéan resident since the last Ice Age before it was reintroduced after the park was created. It is now widespread.

Park birds include the lammergeier or bearded vulture. These huge birds – the wing span is up to 10ft/3m – are rare, a consequence of their specialist feeding habits. They feed almost exclusively on bones, which they carry high and drop, hoping to break them and so expose the marrow. Egyptian and griffon vultures are also found here.

Other park species include the natterjack toad, the tadpoles of which often fail to complete their metamorphosis to adult toads during the relatively short Pyrénéan summer and so overwinter as tadpoles, completing the change the following year.

There is also a superb collection of over 150 alpine plant species for the spring walker to enjoy, around 12 per cent of which are endemic, these including Pyrénéan iris, white Pyrénéan buttercups, Pyrénéan saxifrage and the pale lilac Pyrénéan thistle.

Butterflies include two swallowtails and two apollos, as well as the Gavarnie blue, which is found only in the park and the Picos de Europa, and the rare glandon blue, a high-altitude species.

The Spanish Parque Nacional de Ordesa y Monte Perdido was created in 1918 and was enlarged to 61 sq. miles (156 sq. km) in 1982. Despite the arid climate and karst scenery (i.e. the lack of surface water) of the park it has a surprisingly lush vegetation, with beech and oak trees at lower elevations and box and black pine higher up. There is also an excellent collection of alpine plant species. The park's fauna is similar to that of the contiguous French park. One important addition is the now very rare Pyrénéan ibex, a subspecies of the Spanish ibex. Reptiles include the equally rare Iberian rock lizard.

Both the HRP and GR11 touch Spain's Parque National d'Aigüestortes i Estany de Sant Maurici. It covers 55 sq. miles (140 sq. km) of high mountain and coniferous forest, and is home to many Pyrénéan mammal and bird species. The latter include not only the vultures for which the mountains are famous but alpine accentor, citril finch and crag martins.

In addition to the National Parks, the walking routes pass through several nature reserves, as mentioned above. GR10 also edges the eastern boundary of the nature reserve around the granite Pic de Néouvielle, which includes the highest black pine forest in Europe.

LEFT Wall lizard.

OPPOSITE
ABOVE Lammergeier.
BELOW LEFT Cinnibar moth on Pyrénéan scabious.
BELOW RIGHT Pyrénéan gentian.

Château de Peyrepertuse

MASSIF DES CORBIÈRES, FRANCE

Set high on a rocky pinnacle in the mountains to the north-west of Perpignan is the impressive castle of Peyrepertuse, once a retreat of the religious group known as the Cathars. Catharism, which spread through Languedoc – that area of south-west France where the Oc language (now called Provençal) rather than French was spoken – during the twelfth century, is hard to define simply. Its origins – even the origin of 'Cathar' – are still discussed, some authorities seeing elements of Persian beliefs, even of Zoroastrianism and Eastern mysticism as well as a central element of Christianity. But Catharism was at odds with Catholicism. Cathars held that two gods ruled creation: a good god who reigned over the spiritual realm of heaven and an evil god who reigned over all material worlds, including the earth. They believed that Jesus Christ was a spiritual presence on earth (not a material form), sent to show the righteous path to heaven. Cathars rejected Mass, the Old Testament, marriage, burial rituals,

even organized religion, though they did have a priesthood. The priests, or *parfaits* (perfect ones), could be men or women. They wore simple clothes, were celibate, ate a simple diet and, apart from interpreting the Gospels, existed chiefly to carry out the consolamentum, the Cathar baptism. Baptism was necessary to become a *parfait*, as it required foregoing the evil pleasures of the natural world as a preparation for death and heaven. For non-*parfaits* it was therefore performed when the believer was dying.

OPPPOSITE Peyrepertuse castle occupies a long, narrow ridge crest. Be careful – the ridge edges are unprotected and a fall into the valley would undoubtedly be fatal.

BELOW Looking towards the valley walk from the castle.

LEFT With its extraordinary position, Peyrepertuse is the almost perfect castle, but the difficulty of obtaining water meant it was much less impregnable than it appears.

BELOW The lush vegetation of the valley below the castle is ideal for butterflies such as the marbled white (ABOVE).

For the Catholic Church, Catharism was a heresy and, providentially for the king of France, concerns over it arose when there was a political need to subjugate Languedoc. When an envoy sent by the Pope to convert the Cathars was murdered, it was the excuse needed for a Crusade against the Cathars. Beginning in 1209 the Crusade lasted twenty bloody years, with tens of thousands of Languedocians – Cathars and Catholics alike – slaughtered. To escape the slaughter many Cathars retreated to the series of hilltop castles that pepper the Languedoc countryside. That at Peyrepertuse was virtually impregnable, but it was difficult to keep supplied, particularly with water, and so could not survive a persistent siege, and eventually surrendered.

The castle site has been occupied since at least the ninth century, but the ruins that remain are three centuries younger. Built along 900ft (275m) of narrow ridge with huge, sheer cliffs on both sides, the castle is an engineering marvel. It is also impressively dangerous, the site being closed on wet or windy days as in places the rock, polished by countless feet, slopes in two directions at once, and the drops have little or no protection. Clearly health and safety and the blame culture are less prevalent in France than in Britain, the attitude suggesting that anyone stupid enough to risk a fatal fall has only themselves to blame.

After enjoying the castle, descend to the village of Duilhac-sous-Peyrepertuse. Now follow the lane beside the village map board (which has details of the walk). The lane becomes a track and then a footpath bears off left, allowing you to maintain direction, parallel to the D14, to meet the road at the Col de la Croix Dessus. Here, turn right on the signed track for the Moulin de Ribaute. Follow the track, forking right once and then following a path where the track turns sharp right. Walk above the River Verdouble, descending to a point where the old flour mill is visible across the river. Now follow the path west back to the village: a couple of small streams need to be (easily) forded along the way. Finally, climb back to the castle.

Walk Information

Map: IGN 1:25,000 series sheet 2447OT.
Start/Finish: The car park at Peyreperteuse castle. Length: 3 miles (5km). Ascent: 650ft (200m).

Peyrepertuse is on Sentier Cathare, a long-distance path which links the major Cathar sites. Much of the suggested walk follows the *sentier*, and a longer walk along the route can be used to visit Quéribus, another hilltop castle, seen BELOW through the mist of early morning. The two castles are about 7.5 miles (12km) apart.

GR20

CORSICA

To the approaching traveller, Corsica appears as one huge mountain rearing up from the Mediterranean. That view is hardly a novel description of the island, and neither is it, geologically, a very accurate one. The N193/N200 roads, which link the northern coast to the east coast at Aléria, very approximately divide the island into two geological zones. To the west, and also in the Désert des Agriates, which lies east of the N193 close to the northern coast, are crystalline rocks, granites, rhyolite and gabbro, created by a volcanic upheaval eons ago. To the east of the roads and the desert are schists, sedimentary rocks uplifted by the tectonic movements that created the Alps and then metamorphosed under the compression of being thrust against the hard western block. The west coast comprises later alluvial rocks, while at the island's southern tip there is some limestone. These are the basic rocks, the landforms we see having been chiselled by ice, wind and water. The impression of a single mountain is aided by Corsica's size: it is just 114 miles (183km) long and only 52 miles (83km) at its widest, yet has a highest peak, Monte Cinto, that rises to 8,876ft (2,706m).

Corsica is one of the twenty-six *régions* of France (though technically it is actually a *collectivité territoriale*, a status which gives it

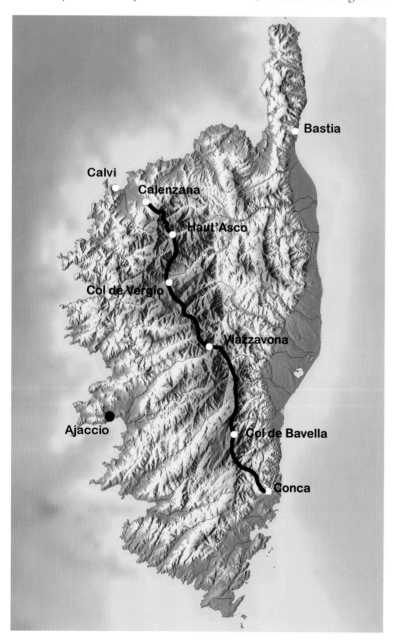

greater powers than those of the mainland *régions*), but, as Alexandre Dumas said, it may be French, but it is far from being France. After periods of being a Greek colony and then part of the Roman Empire, the island became a pawn in the conflicts between Italian city states – not surprisingly, as it is only 56 miles (90km) from Italy (but 106 miles (170km) from France). By 1729 it had been part of the Genoese Republic for almost 400 years. In that year the Corsicans, then as now fiercely independent, began a struggle that culminated, in 1755, in the creation of the Corsican Republic. But the Genoese retained a foothold on the island, merchants from the city living in the ports and the Genoese still proclaiming ownership (out of the hearing of the locals). In 1768 the Genoese secretly sold the island to France. War followed, but it was a war the islanders could not hope to win, and Corsica became a part of France in 1770.

Today the Corsicans continue to maintain a certain distance from France. A well-known saying is *primu corsu, franchese dopu*, 'Corsican first, French second'; and the Testa di Moru, a black Moor's head sporting a white bandanna, set on a white background, the official standard of the Corsican Republic, is still seen across the island. Ironically, in view of its feelings towards France (in a recent poll, less than 25 per cent of Corsicans felt themselves to be more French than Corsican), one of the most famous of all 'Frenchmen', Napoléon Bonaparte, was Corsican, having been born in Ajaccio in 1769.

A coastal plain and valleys carved by rivers swollen by the spring melt of winter snows are the only low relief from the peaks of the high interior. Those peaks are at their highest in a narrow band that stretches north–west to south–east across the island. It is this band – which is not continuous, deep valleys being carved through it in many places – that GR20 takes.

The route offers the walker an amazing contrast. On the coast, where the walk starts and ends, Corsica is a Mediterranean holiday paradise. Up in the hills, it is a rugged wilderness of jagged peaks and deep, forested valleys. The walk is hard going: the 110 mile (170km) route involves 34,500ft (10,500m) of ascent and descent, while the climate, though admirable for a beach holiday, is less palatable for the average walker, requiring a lot of drinking water to be carried to compensate for the dehydration brought on by high temperatures, sunshine and uphill effort. It is claimed that 50 per cent of those who set out on the walk with the intention of completing it fail, many during/after the first hard days. For those who succeed, this is an incomparable walk, one of the very best.

The walk starts in Calenzana, a small town just a few kilometres from Calvi in the north-east of the island. In 1732 the town was the scene of a bloody battle when German mercenaries hired by the Holy Roman Emperor, Charles VI, to support the Genoese were routed by a handful of Corsicans, aided by the townspeople. The Corsicans allowed the invaders into the town, effectively corralling them in the narrow streets, and then showered them with everything from burning torches to beehives. The campanile beside the church in the main square was built to commemorate the victory and many of the Genoese dead, numbering perhaps 200, are buried near by. From the main square you take a well-signed, meandering path to the Oratoire Saint Antoine, the official start.

Start early to avoid the heat of the day on the hardest ascent. The walk starts as it means to continue, with a steep, rugged path – an old

mule track – that rises between old walls and then passes through maquis to reach a path junction. A variant through Bonifatu bears right here, while the main path takes a zigzag route as it climbs through pines/maquis, a cable aiding progress through a boulder section (take care, slippery when wet) before you reach Refuge de l'Orto di u Piobbu (5,150ft/1,570m). This first stage covers only about 6 miles (10km), but involves 4,260ft (1,300m) of climbing.

Day two is a little easier, climbing to the Bocca Piccaia (6,306ft/1,950m) with fine views of Monte Corona. Further on, beyond Bocca d'Avartoli, Monte Cinto and other jagged peaks come into view, competing with the view down dizzying rock faces to the Ladroncellu valley. To finish the day, care is needed on the steep and loose final descent to the often crowded Refuge de Carrozzu. From the refuge there is another long climb, slippery after rain and with occasional cables for aid, to a sharp ridge and the Lavu di a Muvrella, a crystal-clear lake. The clarity is due to the lack of aquatic life; the lake freezes solid in winter, which prevents life from gaining a 'foothold'. The water is unfit for humans to drink, but *muvra*, the Corsican mouflon (the name muvrella means 'young muvra'), use it regularly, usually at dusk. Camping here is strictly forbidden because that would prevent the mouflon, who are shy animals, approaching and so deny them the water, which could be catastrophic. So it is best not to linger. The route continues past an outcrop shaped like a native American's head, complete with feathered headdress, and up to the Bocca de Stagnu (6,593ft/2,010m), from where Monte Cinto, straight ahead,

ABOVE GR20 starts with a steep climb up a rugged path to reach open hillside and mountain views.

RIGHT On the chains of the Cirque de Solitude.

LEFT Looking back towards the Refuge de Ciottulu a i Mori, with Capu Tafunata to the left, and Paglia Orba to the right.
BELOW The valley below the Col de Vergio.

dominates the view. Then it descends steeply to Haut'Asco (4,664ft/1,422m), the usual starting point for ascents of Corsica's highest peak. The peak's name translates as 'encircled', the mountain being surrounded by lower summits.

Haut'Asco is an old ski centre with a full range of facilities. It is also reachable by road, one of the handful of places where GR20 meets tarmac. From it the route climbs again, this time with the peaks of the Cirque de Trimbolacciu providing the view when gaps in the pine forest allow. Beyond the charred remains of the Refuge d'Altore, destroyed by fire in 1982, the climb steepens to reach the edge of E Cascettoni, more often known as the Cirque de Solitude. During the walking season this famous feature offers anything but solitude, the steep, chain-aided descent of 660ft (200m) and similar climb out usually being crowded. Crowds also mean that traversing the cirque takes time, as there is only one route, and if walkers are going both ways, frequent delays. From the exit col (Bocca Minuta, at

7,275ft/2,218m) there are terrific views to the peaks you will cross in a few days; then there is a straightforward descent to Refuge Tighiettu or, further on, the Bergeries de Vallone, a smaller, more homely spot run by a local shepherd (a *bergerie* being a simple, stone-built shepherd's hut).

The going is easier now, through pine forest, then juniper and broom, before a stiff climb to the beautifully sited Refuge de Ciottulu a i Moro. Juniper was much prized by Corsicans, who made excellent kitchen utensils from its wood. They also used the wood to make a bucket which the priest placed ceremonially on the bride's head to symbolize the burden of marriage, of being a good wife and mother, that would weigh her down. For the walker juniper can also be a burden, for the dwarf variety on higher ground is a low, spreading plant whose thorns scratch unprotected legs.

Those who stopped at the shepherd's hut may have energy to spare and can miss the refuge on a variant that descends into the wooded

Golu valley. A little further on there is another choice, depending on where you intend to spend the night. If you have bypassed the Ciuttulu refuge you can continue into the valley to reach the huge, unsightly, but entirely adequate Castellu di Vergio. If you have had a short day and stayed at Ciuttulu, you can miss the 'castle' by bearing right by the shepherd's huts on a track, often well populated, which leads to the huge statue of the Virgin at the Col de Vergio. The car park here explains the populated track. To continue, cross the road and take the track ahead to a now-desolate ski-tow – Castellu di Vergio was built as a ski centre, but global warming means fewer snowy days. Continue over the crest ahead (Capu â Ruja), and on to Bocca San Pedro (4,763ft/1,452m), where you rejoin the official route.

You now climb easily to the delightful Lac di Nino, popular with fishermen after the lake's abundant Corsican trout. It is forbidden to camp at the lake as the environment – with peaty areas between the small pools and linking streams, known as *pozzi* (*pozzines* in French) – is delicate. The nitrogen-poor soil of the *pozzines* means that insectivorous plants thrive: not only the common sundew, but two endemic forms, *Drosera corsica*, a subspecies of the sundew, and the butterwort *Pinguicula corsica*. Further on, the Bergeries de Vaccaghia are famous for their ewe's cheese, which comes in several forms, all equally pungent, and the tastiest capable of removing the skin from the taster's throat. As one nineteenth-century visitor remarked, 'He who has not tasted it does not know the island.' It is possible to stay at the huts, but you may wish to continue to the Refuge de Manganu, a busy place but a great viewpoint.

GR20 now heads for the high hills again, climbing steadily to the Brèche du Capitellu (7,298ft/2,225m), a gash in the ridge, beyond

ABOVE Lac de Nino.

RIGHT An indication of the ferocity of winter winds on the Bocca San Pedru (Col de St Pierre).

ABOVE Looking towards Monte d'Oro from the forest path above the Col de Vizzavona.
BELOW The Aiguilles de Bavella.
RIGHT On the aided section of the walk between the Aiguilles de Bavella and the Col de Bavella. The descending walker is heading towards the Aiguilles.

The Col de Bavella.

which there is a wonderful view down to the Capitellu and Melu Lakes. The walking here is impressive – both the view and the track – though the descent from the pass is steep. There is another good viewpoint at the Bocca Muzzella before a descent to Refuge de Petra Piana (the 'flat rock' refuge, named for the hut's position), a base for climbing Monte Rotondo (8,600ft/2,622m), Corsica's second highest peak.

The route now offers high- and low-level variants to reach the Refuge de l'Onda. The high-level route is more in keeping with the overall GR, but holds snow late into the summer and is windswept, making a crossing in bad weather inadvisable: ask the guardian at Petra Piana if you are in any doubt. From Refuge de l'Onda, after a sharp climb to the Crête de Muratello (6,888ft/2,100m), there are again variant routes. A high-level route goes over Monte d'Oro (at 7,836ft (2,389m) Corsica's fifth highest summit), but has little other merit and means a descent of over 4,600ft (1,400m) to Vizzavona.

Even the usually preferred route, which descends through boulder-strewn woodland, involves almost 4,000ft (1,200m) of descent, but it has the advantage of passing the famous Cascades des Anglais, a series of short waterfalls into clear pools (best early in the season, as the stream volume reduces appreciably in summer).

There are hotels at Vizzavona, and rather less agreeable facilities at the train station to the left. The train line between Ajaccio and Bastia was built at the end of the nineteenth century and was soon popular with the English wintering at the two towns, Vizzavona making a

pleasant, airy day trip. The money the English brought persuaded the locals to change the name of the major local attraction, the waterfalls and pools on the Agnone stream having formerly been the Cascades des Italiens. As Vizzavona is more or less the halfway stage of the GR, you can use the train to split your completion of the route.

From the station, GR20 continues through forest to another winter sports centre (E' Capannelle), which has seen better days but is a handy refuge. From it a section of level and gently downhill walking leads to the Col de Verde, another of the few road crossings, and its refuge, with a high-level variant that seeks alpine rather than rural scenery by climbing Monte Renoso (7,715ft/2,352m) but should not be attempted in poor weather as finding the waymarking cairns requires good visibility.

From Col de Verde, the route climbs past Refuge di Prati, and then follows the island's watershed. This is a fabulous section of walking along an undulating ridge (though 'undulating' might be too flimsy a word for a ridge that involves 1,500ft (450m) descents and ascents, with sharp climbs on both, as well as lesser undulations), occasionally slipping off the ridge to outflank rock gendarmes. At the Bocca di Laparo, there is a route that descends, right, to the village of Cozzano, but walkers who have overnighted at the Col de Verde refuge should be able to able to reach Refuge d'Usciolu. To be sure, you need a *petra quadrata*, a magical stone sought by early Corsicans, who believed it offered the carrier immunity to fatigue while crossing the mountains with their interminable ups and downs. Another Corsican idea, according to a nineteenth-century writer, was that a stone tied to the left leg, above the knee, allowed walking without tiring.

Alpine, and is distinctly more alpine, climbing to the Bocca di u Pargulu (5,451ft/1,662m) by outflanking the Bavella *aiguilles* and then descending to where a chain aids a short climb. The going is easier now as you reach a final pass that reveals the Col de Bavella, which is a hive of activity on most sunny days. The Variante can be tricky in wet weather, but has no real difficulties.

At the col there is a fine restaurant and a statue of Notre Dame de la Neige (Our Lady of the Snow). The main difficulties of the route are now, forested tracks taking you on an up-and-down route to Refuge de Paliri. From there it is almost all downhill, though there are final flourishes of uphill walking before the final descent to Conca. Unpretentious and picturesque, the village lacks a little as the terminus of a magnificent walk, but those staying at the La Tonnelle *gîte d'étape* will find the owner's minibus a handy way to reach one of Corsica's fine south-eastern beaches for a paddle in the warm Mediterranean – a fitting finale.

LEFT Descending from the Col de Bavella.
BELOW Opuntia cactus.

OPPOSITE Maquis, which can make life difficult for the off-route walker.

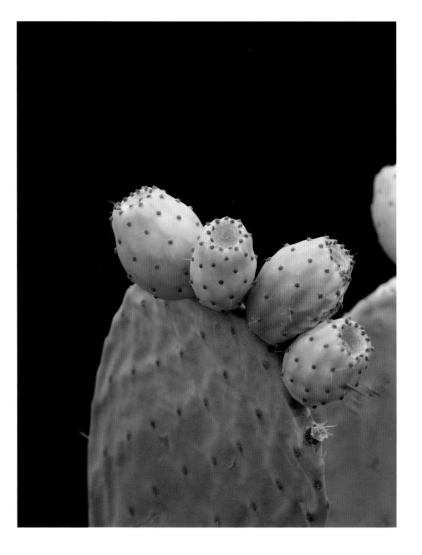

On the ridge you negotiate a paint-blob-marked, apparently unlikely and certainly ingenious route that threads around pinnacles and boulders on a sharp ridge and then crosses a high, grassy plateau once populated by hundreds of sheep, herded here during the annual transhumance. Today the transhumance – the moving of the animals from low-level winter pasture (the *piaghja*) to high-level summer forage (the *muntaga*) – is much reduced, though it is still possible to meet flocks on the move. The plateau is the only place on the island where an endemic member of the buttercup family, the pale lilac Corsican aconite, grows. Next you climb to Monte Incudine (7,000ft/2,134m), an excellent viewpoint, especially of the Aiguilles de Bavella, the next objective, and descend to Refuge d'Asinao.

You can avoid the Aiguilles de Bavella by bearing right – follow the yellow waymarkers – soon after leaving the refuge and taking a route that descends the Asinao valley. The main route is called the Variante

Travel

By air There are regular flights to Nice, many budget airlines catering for travellers to the Côte d'Azur. There are then regular flights from Nice to Ajaccio, Bastia and Calvi.

By sea There are regular all-year vehicle and passenger ferry services to Corsica from Marseille and Nice, and a summer service from Toulon. There are also services from several Italian ports. The ferries serve Ajaccio, Bastia and Calvi. The fastest service is the Corsica Ferries hydrofoil from Nice.

Calenzana and Conca It is easier to get to Calenzana from Calvi than from either Ajaccio or Bastia. From the latter use the train to reach Calvi, and then the local bus that links the town to Calenzana. Getting to/from Conca is more complicated. As noted above, the La Tonnelle *gîte d'étape* minibus is a big aid to walkers, transporting them to Ste-Lucie-de-Porto-Vecchio, from where buses link to Bastia, or to Porto-Vecchio for buses to Ajaccio. Walkers aiming for Conca will probably need a taxi from either town unless they contact La Tonnelle to organize collection.

Maps and guides

GR20-Corsica: The High Level Route, Paddy Dillon, Cicerone.
Corsica Trekking: GR20, David Abram, Trailblazer.

Both are excellent; Abram's is slightly newer (published 2008).

IGN produce two maps at 1:100,000 which cover the whole of Corsica, sheets 73 and 74. Though the scale is smaller than that walkers will be used to, the maps are perfectly adequate when used in conjunction with one of the excellent guides to the route. Walkers wanting more detail can invest in the required maps from IGN's 1:25,000 scale maps, nineteen of which cover the island.

Waymarking

GR20 is superbly waymarked throughout with the standard red and white flashes on trees, rocks, etc., as well as specific signs. Variants to the route are marked in yellow. In mountain areas where snow might linger and obscure the paint, cairns are used.

Accommodation

It is possible, by planning very carefully, to complete the route using the refuges strategically placed along it. However, some of the refuges get crowded, and walkers who take minimal camping equipment will find it useful: it is never much of a problem to find meals and drinks at the refuges, but the ability to make a simple meal can prove equally useful. In general, tents can be pitched anywhere, but many walkers make do with a sleeping bag, finding a sheltered spot to spend the night. If the night is wind free and starlit, bivouacing is a great idea. If it rains and blows a gale, it is much less fun and takes the edge off the entire expedition.

Equipment

GR20 can be walked in its entirety in shorts and T-shirt. But if the weather is mischievous you will need waterproofs and even a fleece jacket and windproof jacket on the windswept higher sections.

Climate

Corsica has hot dry summers and cool, wet winters, the rain falling as snow on the high peaks. From May to September, the walker will likely have rain-free days, but temperatures can rise to 86°F/30°C and more, and even at altitude the unshaded sun can be roasting. But summer storms are possible, these often including thunder and lightning, so you must be prepared. Wind is also a problem, particularly towards the southern end of the route as it nears the sea.

Interestingly, GR20 and the refuges are most crowded at the height of summer, walkers from southern Europe finding the heat less trying than those from the north. North European walkers will find spring (May/early June) and late summer (September, when the refuges are still open) more agreeable, when the refuge crowds have either yet to arrive or already gone.

Hazards

The chief hazard will be the heat and its attendant dehydration. Do not scrimp on carrying water: 3 litres is a minimum daily requirement, so drink as much as you can at start of day, top up water bottles, CamelBak, etc. whenever the opportunity presents itself, and drink as much as you can at refuges you pass along the way. In general Corsican spring water is potable, but adding a couple of water purifiers to your bottle is always a good idea.

As much of the walking will be in direct sunlight, sun block is essential. Bear in mind when buying supplies that sweat is likely to wash it off in a few hours of hard uphill slogging.

Corsica has only two snakes. One is the harmless grass snake, which is found throughout Europe. The other is the western whip snake, a large (to 6ft/2m), slender, vividly marked (yellow/dark green) reptile which can occur at altitudes up to about 5,000ft (1,500m). The whip snake is very aggressive if disturbed, and will bite long and hard if it can. Though not venomous, the bite is very nasty and will need medical attention.

National Parks and Wildlife

Virtually the entire GR20 lies within the Parc Naturel Régional de Corse, set up to protect a unique ecosystem which includes a host of endemic species. The park includes the Scandola Peninsula and the waters of the adjacent Golfe de Girolata and Golfe de Porto, which lie between Ajaccio and Calvi (and are well off the route).

The island's ecology shows three diverse zones: a coastal belt lying below 2,000ft (610m) where summer temperatures are highest and winters are warmest; a montane zone at elevations of 2,000–6,000ft (600–1,800m) where both broadleaf and conifer forests abound; and an alpine zone above 6,000ft (1,800m) where vegetation is much scarcer. Walkers will spend almost no time in the lowest zone, though those who have days at the end of the trek will likely visit the coast. The coastal plain is one of the last strongholds of Hermann's tortoise, though it is much easier to see the animal at the tortoise sanctuary on the N193 a few kilometres out of Ajaccio. Other rare Corsican reptiles include the tiny (about 1½in/4cm, but with a long tail) brown Pygmy algyroides, the much larger (about 8in/20cm including tail) yellow-green Bedriaga's rock lizard, which is found to 6,600ft (2,000m), and the beautifully coloured (green-brown) Tyrrhenian wall lizard, all of which are found only on the island and neighbouring Sardinia.

Corsica has several endemic mammals. The Corsican mouflon (*murva*) was both hunted and had to compete for forage with domestic animals, resulting in a decrease in numbers. Now fully protected, the population is thought to be about 600. The Corsican red deer was also overhunted and is now very rare, the population being no more than a few dozen. The Corsican dormouse is believed to be a subspecies of the edible dormouse. There is also an endemic bird, the Corsican nuthatch, though walkers are more likely to look for golden eagles and lammergeiers, both of which may be seen among the high peaks.

Walkers will become familiar with maquis on lower sections of the walk, a tangle of juniper, broom and aromatic shrubs. The thickest, most impenetrable maquis was used as a hiding place for resistance fighters during the Second World War, which explains the use of the word for the French Resistance movement. You will also become familiar with Corsican forests, which include holm and cork oaks, and silver birch. Of the conifers the dominant form is the Corsican pine (*Pinus laricio*, a form of black pine), which grows to a height of 160ft (50m) and is so straight it was used for the masts of sailing ships.

The plant life supports many beautiful butterflies, but the insect with which you will become most familiar is the pine processionary moth, though you are unlikely to actually see it. The moth lays eggs in a silken tent and the caterpillars emerge from it each evening – in the procession of the name – to feed on pine needles. When ready for pupation the caterpillars process during the day to find suitable sites. The silken tents are a common sight in the island's pine forests. The caterpillars – their marching activities giving them the French name *chenilles processionnaires* – are a serious pest to the trees.

TOP Wild crocus.

ABOVE Sowbread (*Cyclamen hederifolium*).

ABOVE LEFT Silk tent of pine processionary moth on Corsican black pine.

BELOW LEFT Hermann's tortoise.

BELOW RIGHT Edible frog. Both tortoise and frog are easier to find at the sanctuary close to Ajaccio.

OPPOSITE

ABOVE LEFT Reticulated male Tyrrhenian wall lizard.

BELOW LEFT Bedriaga's rock lizard.

RIGHT Italian wall lizard.

The Samaria Gorge

CRETE, GREECE

Famous for its archaeological remains, particularly at Knossos, and as a holiday resort for lovers of sand, sea and sun, Crete seems an unlikely place for walking. But the island has a mountainous heart, with peaks rising to over 7,800ft (2,400m) in the White Mountains. In winter snow falls, turning the mountain summits a true white, but in the glare of summer's sun the glistening limestone is almost as pale. In 1962 the White Mountains were designated Crete's first National Park, though the name the park is more often given is Samaria, referring to its most famous feature.

The Samaria Gorge falls 4,100ft (1,250m) in a distance of 8 miles (13km). That does not sound so steep until you realize that almost the entire height change occurs in the first 3 miles (5km) or so. Beyond the descent, at one point the gorge narrows to just 13ft (4m), hemmed in by sheer cliffs over 1,100ft (350m) high. In winter and spring the river which carved the gorge fills that narrow section, making a traverse impossible, and the walk through it is closed from November until May, reopening only when the water level has subsided sufficiently to allow safe passage. As a result, walkers tackle that knee-attacking descent during the heat of summer. The Samaria Gorge can therefore be a fatiguing excursion, but in exchange it offers wonderful rock scenery, particularly where the strata are wildly contorted or water-eroded, plant life very different from that of the mountains of mainland Europe and a return journey that can be as exciting as the walk itself.

The top of the gorge is a short distance from the village of Omalos. Walkers usually start early from Xyloskala, the entrance point to the

OPPOSITE The tightest part of the gorge.

BELOW An early start avoids the most open section of the gorge being reached in the heat of the day, and allows a stunning view from the start point as the sun rises.

National Park, where a small fee is payable. Keep your ticket, as you will need to surrender it at the final barrier. The name of the start point derives from 'wooden staircase', describing the makeshift ladders ancient dwellers in the gorge made of various pieces of wood and used to descend the steeper section. Today the descent is better engineered, though there are still wooden rails to aid walkers. Take care here: the gravel of the path can be loose, and the larger flat stones are polished by the passage of feet and the relentless summer sun, so slips and falls are frequent, especially among elderly or inexperienced walkers caught out by the effort of the continuous descent. Fatigue is not helped by the kilometre markers placed beside the path, which seem to arrive after much too long an interval.

After 2km the steepest section of the path has been completed, and a shallower descent brings you to Agios Nikolaos (at 4km), a tiny church sited among cypress, Calabrian pine and Palestine oak. Some of the cypresses, gnarled by countless hard winters and hot summers, are believed to be more than a thousand years old. Near by is a cave now called Demonospilios (Devil's Cave), which is believed to have been a temple of Apollo at the height of the Greek civilization. In one version of a Greek legend, this spot was the birthplace of Diana Britomartis, the goddess of hunting.

You now reach the river, which the flat path crosses several times on the way to Samaria, the ancient gorge village (7km). As this is about

halfway along the walk, there are likely to be many walkers resting and eating here, a fact which has led the Cretan wild goat (especially young animals) to favour the area, eager to share the odd sandwich. This goat (*Capra aegagrus*) is confined to Crete (where the main population is around Samaria) and a handful of smaller islands, but its true origins are disputed, some authorities believing it is actually a feral animal introduced perhaps several thousand years ago. Interbreeding with domestic goats has also led some to question whether there are any longer any pure-bred goats on the island. Known locally as kri-kri, the goats tend to be much smaller and lighter than the ibex of the Alps.

The village itself was occupied until 1962, when the creation of the National Park meant enforced departure for the few people who remained. Villagers kept cattle and bees, their honey being prized across the island, and operated a small sawmill producing high-quality timber. It was a hard life, as winter cut the settlement off from the coast for several months, making timber export impossible.

From the village the walk enters its most exciting stage. After a wide valley section – there is an abundance of wild flowers here: early in the season look out especially for orchids, several of which are endemic and extremely beautiful – the gorge narrows. The occasional sign warns of falling rocks – bear in mind they may be arriving from 1,500ft (500m) above – so it is best not to linger too long admiring the rock strata. At Sidiroportes (11km), the Castle Gates, the gorge is at its

narrowest. Throughout history Samaria has been used as an enclave by Cretans resisting attempts by foreigners to conquer the island. Turkish invaders never managed to break through the gates here, as a small force was capable of holding off a much larger one. During the Second World War, the Greek king and his government used the gorge as a means of escape, and the Germans never managed to eradicate the partisans who sheltered here.

Progress in the narrowest section of the gorge is occasionally aided by a makeshift wooden walkway so that visitors can remain dry shod; it can also be slow, as day visitors arriving from the seaward side to observe the narrow gorge add to those admiring the steep walls. But soon the gorge opens out again, and you reach the exit, where tickets are surrendered. Beyond, you pass the old village of Agia Roumeli to reach the new village and the sea.

To return to the start, if your plan is not to reverse the walk (most walkers do not), you must use a ferry. Boats link to Hóra Sfakion, from where transport to Chania is readily available (walkers staying there can buy an inclusive ticket). Private walkers who have stayed at Omalos can instead take the ferry west to Sougia, from where a taxi will transport you back to the village. Depending on the driver (and there appeared to be only one in 2007), the journey may be both fast and hair-raising.

Walk information

Map: not necessary, as the route is very clear. Freytag & Berndt produce a 1:50,000 hiking map of Crete (WKGR1) which includes the gorge. An alternative is the excellent guide *Follow Us in the Gorge of Samaria* by Alibertis Antonis, which includes a map and some interesting information.
Start: Xyloskala. Finish: Agia Roumeli. Length: 10 miles (16km). No ascent, but 4,100ft (1,250m) of descent.

RIGHT ABOVE *Drakondia* is the local name for the plant known in English as dragon lily or dragon arum. It is one of the most spectacular of the flowers found in the gorge.
RIGHT BELOW A female kri-kri.

OPPOSITE Contorted rock strata near the tightest part of the gorge.

GR5

FRANCE

The European Alps are a reminder of a now long-gone sea, the Tethys Ocean, which once separated Africa and Europe. When tectonic activity made the continents collide, the ocean disappeared and the Alps were formed from the crumpled land of the collision zone. In more scientific terms, the collision created huge folds (nappes) which emerged from the ocean and were pushed north. Their sliding caused the faults that separate the mountain blocks, exposing crystalline rocks from deep beneath the water which formed the higher peaks such as Mont Blanc and the Matterhorn. The structure of the mountains is, in one sense, straightforward: an arc of high peaks rises from the Mediterranean near the Côte d'Azur in France and curves north-east to encompass not only the Alps but also the Dolomites, the mountains of the Balkans, the Carpathians and the Caucasus. Geologically, however, the mountain chain is complex, a mix of sedimentary, intrusive and metamorphic rocks which can keep a field worker occupied for a lifetime.

As one might expect, Europe's highest Alps attract not only climbers but walkers. The Tour de Mont Blanc is famous across the walking world, its acronym TMB equally well known. The linking route between the Continent's highest peak (if Elbrus' claim to that title is ignored) and the Matterhorn, the Continent's most recognizable peak, is almost as well known, offering both summer and winter options. Less well known, but deserving a better audience, is the Tour of the Matterhorn.

All three routes make a claim to being among the best walking routes in Europe. But another route makes, in my view, an even stronger claim. Making its way from Lac Léman to the Mediterranean, GR5 passes through, or runs close to, all the French alpine areas: Mont Blanc, the Vanoise, the Ecrins and the Alpes-Maritimes. The description below concentrates on GR5, but brief details are also given on the other high-peak routes.

Technically GR5 links the North Sea to the Mediterranean, the true start being on the Dutch coast, but for the mountain walker the start is Lac Léman, or alternatively Thonon-les-Bains or St Gingolph. The latter is the continuation of the full route, which swings around the northern and eastern shores of the lake. The St Gingolph start also allows you to reach the mountains early, the walk starting out exactly as it means to go on, by climbing to the Col de Bise (6,281ft/1,915m), a climb of almost 5,000ft (1,500m) in the first 6 miles (10km). The route stays high before descending to La Chapelle d'Abondance, where most walkers spend their first night, exhilarated by the walk and the views, and contemplating the remaining 400 miles (650km) of walking and 130,000ft (40,000m) of climbing that lie ahead.

The views improve, Mont Blanc and its satellites being visible from the top of the long climb to Les Mattes (7,334ft/1,930m). The route now stays high, crossing from France into Switzerland and following an undulating route across lovely, flower-dotted alp, though with occasionally steep path sections. The view is dominated by the Dents Blanche, with the Dents du Midi to the east, as you descend gently back into France and then down to the village of Samoëns, its attractive old heart surrounded by much less appealing modern buildings.

From the village the route makes an adventurous passage of the Gorges des Tines with ladders at first, and then, later, cables to aid progress. It continues past the impressive Cascade de Rouget, and climbs over the Col d'Anterne and then to the route's first significant

summit, Le Brévent (8,282ft/2,525m). The summit boasts a café/restaurant and a terrace from where there is arguably the best view of Mont Blanc and neighbouring peaks. At the summit GR5 is joined by the TMB. Neither route actually visits Chamonix, at the base of the mountain; the walker has the choice of a fine bird's-eye view of this famous alpine centre or of using the cable car to visit it, either for a

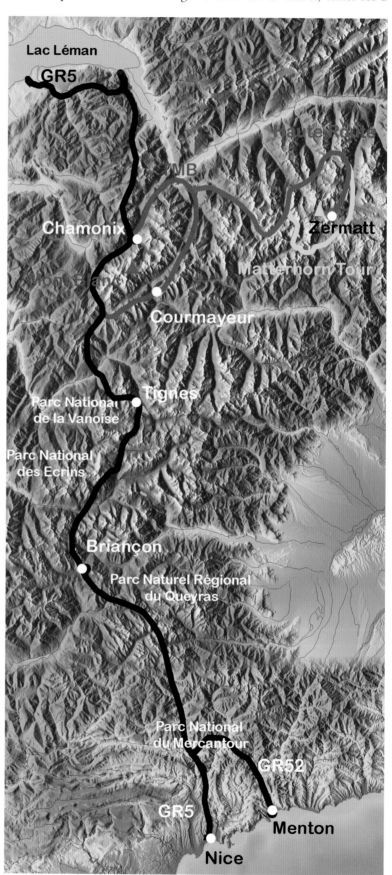

few hours or as an overnight stop. Either way a visit is worthwhile, the town being the premier French alpine resort, comparable with Zermatt or Cortina d'Ampezzo in terms of history and romantic allure.

The tiny village of Chamonix was 'discovered' in the nineteenth century by British tourists keen to see Mont Blanc and the nearby Mer de Glace, but only after the Swiss scientist Horace-Bénédict de Saussure, who had also come to observe Mont Blanc, offered a reward to the first man to reach the summit. The offer, made in 1760, was substantial, but it was not until 1775 that anyone made a serious attempt to take up de Saussure's challenge. The attempt failed, and it was a further eleven years before the first ascent. In 1786 two Chamonix residents, Dr Michel-Gabriele Paccard and Jacques Balmat, reached the summit, each having failed several times in the previous three years. The aftermath of the first ascent was not pleasant. Balmat claimed rather more credit than seems to have been due to him: Paccard, a modest man, stood by as his position diminished from partner to minor supporting role. Balmat was fêted throughout Europe; Paccard was all but forgotten. In Chamonix a statue shows Balmat indicating the route to the summit for de Saussure. Not until the 200th anniversary of the first ascent was a statue of Paccard raised (though a bust had been placed in the town in 1932).

In the wake of Mont Blanc's ascent mountaineering became popular, particularly among the British gentry, who had both time and the money to employ local guides to help them explore and climb. As a result, the Compagnie des Guides de Chamonix was formed in 1821: this comprised local men and held a monopoly on guiding from the town for seventy years, until the requirement to hold guiding qualifications replaced mere residency. Chamonix remains one of the foremost climbing centres in the Alps, with aspirants arriving to take on the faces of Mont Blanc, Le Grand Capuchin, the Drus and the Grandes Jorasses among others. The town has also developed as a thriving winter sports centre. The 1924 Winter Olympics were held here.

From Le Brévent, GR5 and the TMB descend together to Les Houches, a tidy village that has become established as a winter sports centre with its own character, rather than existing as an overflow of nearby Chamonix. GR5 and the TMB stay together from the village, each offering two variants, the better of which, weather permitting, is a high-level option climbing to the Col de Voza and continuing, with a stupendous view of the Glacier de Bionnassay and the Aiguille de Bionnassay, to the Col de Tricot. From the col a steep path descends to reach an easier forest trail which you follow to Les Contamines-Montjoie.

From the village, the routes again coincide, following an old salt route through fine woodland, and then reaching wilder country and the Col du Bonhomme (7,849ft/2,329m). Care is needed on the final part of the ascent to the col, as snow can lie late into the summer. From the col the routes climb to the Refuge de la Croix du Bonhomme, where they part company. While the TMB heads south-east, the GR5 heads south-west along a notoriously muddy track, with duckboards to assist in places, and then climbs to the Col du Bresson (8,111ft/2,473m). There is a fine view of the Pointe de Presset (9,050ft/2,759m) on the ascent, and another of the rock candle of La Pierra Menta (8,902ft/2,714m) on the way down to the village of Valezan. There are two variants from here, one heading for Landry and

Pointe d'Anterne above Lac d'Anterne, to the south of Sixt-Fer-à-Cheval.

ABOVE A ladder helps the walker on the last stage to Le Brévent.
LEFT A magnificent view of Mont Blanc awaits walkers as they round Le Brévent.

then passing the now-derelict French mining school built on the site of old lead and silver mines, the other heading directly for the high peaks of the Vanoise. They soon meet, and the route then climbs steadily to reach the boundary of the Vanoise National Park and the gloriously positioned Refuge d'Entre le Lac, set beside a pretty lake and surrounded by impressive peaks.

Beyond the refuge you have a choice, the first of several variants that allow a thorough exploration of the National Park. GR5 follows an undulating route through fine country to reach the famous ski resort of Val d'Isere, while a variant (GR55) takes a higher-level route. For those following GR5 another variant is offered further on.

GR5 climbs to Lac de Grattaleu, which is overlooked by rugged peaks, its shore covered with dense patches of cottongrass with occasional plants of the much rarer two-coloured sedge. Then it descends to Tignes-le-Lac, one of the five ski resorts that comprise the Tignes ski area. The original village of Tignes was submerged beneath the waters of Lac du Chevril when the dam for the hydro-electric power station was constructed in 1952; the new village offers year-round glacier skiing but little to detain the student of architecture. Val d'Isere is a more picturesque village, with a fine old centre; today it is one of the most famous ski resorts in Europe with a vast infrastructure of lifts and runs.

Having soaked up the (rather rich) atmosphere of Val d'Isere you will be keen to move on, following an old road over the Col de l'Iseran (9,086ft/2,770m) and descending through wild, beautiful country near the Pont de la Neige to re-enter the National Park (which, unsurprisingly, has avoided the ski area). There are two variants, with

ABOVE Eighteenth-century lithograph of Horace-Bénédict de Saussure's team ascending Mont Blanc in August 1787, the third ascent of the peak.

LEFT Jacques Balmat points out the route to the summit for de Saussure in a statue at the heart of Chamonix.

little to choose between them, before you reach Bessans, beyond which there is a real choice.

GR5E follows a low-level route to Modane, staying close to the Arc River as it flows through gentle, wooded country. The route passes through Lanslebourg-Mont-Cenis, a neat town. You are walking in the footsteps of history here: Hannibal (and his elephants) probably passed this way in AD 218 on his way to Rome.

Mountain lovers will prefer the true route of GR5, which heads west along the edge of the National Park and then turns north into the valley of the Doron, staying between 6,500ft and 8,000ft (about 2,000m–2,500m) all the way to the Refuge du Plan du Lac, with wonderful views throughout. Beyond the refuge the route turns south along the other side of the Doron valley, and then contours around lakes before dropping down to the Arc valley and Mondane.

At Mondane the two GR variants meet GR55, which has traced a high-level route (i.e. an even more mountainous way) through the Vanoise. Walkers on all the variants will find Mondane a useful place with a railway station and a full range of services. GR5 heads south from the town, climbing steadily across meadows and then through woodland. The route passes the sanctuary church of Notre Dame du Charmaix, built in the fifteenth century to house a Black Virgin, an earlier chapel on the spot having become ruinous; the stained marble statue, claimed to have been made in the fifth century, had been

originally set up in a nearby cave and attracted pilgrims for centuries. The route climbs out of the woodland and through marvellous mountain scenery, with the high ridge to Mont Thabor (10,434ft/3,181m) to the west and the France–Italy border ridge to the east. The Col de la Vallée Étroite (7,984ft/2,434m) formerly stood on the border between the two countries, the ownership of the land west of the current border having had a complicated history. It was part of the independent state of Savoy, then part of the kingdom of Sardinia before becoming French. The Roya valley was not transferred to France at that time, as it was the Sardinian king's favourite hunting ground: it became French only in 1947.

To the south, GR5 offers two more variants, GR5B and GR5C, the former offering a brief, but rugged, trip into Italy, the latter a high-level, spectacular (but exposed) way of reaching Briançon. The main route follows a comfortable line, with views west to the Ecrins, a beautiful mountain area now protected by a National Park, to reach Montgenèvre, a ski resort close to the Italian border, and Briançon.

Briançon is the highest town in France and has a long history. The strategic position of the site, at the junction of four valleys, was not lost on those master military technicians the Romans, and was the first settlement in conquered Gaul to be reached on the road from Rome over the Col de Montgenèvre. The town was later heavily fortified by Vauban, Louis XIV's military engineer, as a defence against the Hapsburg Empire. Vauban's works are still the highlight of the town; UNESCO recognized their importance in 2008 by making Briançon a World Heritage Site.

South of Briançon, GR5 soon reaches the Queyras Regional Nature Park, which protects the magnificent scenery you now traverse on the climb to the Col des Ayes (8,125ft/2,477m) and the descent to Brunissard. Beyond the village you pass the spectacular Fort Queyras, another of Vauban's formidable fortresses. Access to the castle can be made by way of a *via ferrata*, a storming which adds a nicely medieval

ABOVE The Queyras Regional Park. The high peak to the right of centre is Mont Viso.
RIGHT One of the rock engravings below Mont Bégo in the Mercantour National Park. The curious face-like carving with extended hands is known as the 'Chief of Tribe'.

OPPOSITE
ABOVE Refuge du Presset and the Aiguille de la Nova from Col de Bresson.
BELOW Dawn light on the Col de Bresson and La Pierre Menta from the Refuge du Presset.

touch to a visit. Ahead now are the peaks of the Mercantour, the next objective on the walk. The route descends to Ceillac, from where it climbs steeply to leave the Queyras Park at the Col Girardin. Downhill from the col some road walking is required before a climb over the Col de Vallonnet leads on to the Col de Mallamort. Between the two cols is the Barraquements de Viraysse, built in the nineteenth century for soldiers who were manning the battery at the summit of the Tête du Viraysse which, at 9,069ft/2,765m, was the highest in France. The barracks are ruinous, though one section is a basic refuge.

After descending to the village of Larche GR5 climbs gently south, entering the Mercantour National Park and approaching Italy at the Pas de la Cavale, a surprisingly rocky pass overlooking country that clearly indicates a change in climate. Here the landscape is influenced by the Mediterranean: a warmer, drier climate alters the vegetation to something closer to the garrigue, which walkers familiar with Provence will recall, while the high-hill animal species, chamois and marmot, are joined by green lizards. For the walker, hot days can be as much a trial as the summer snowstorms to the north, for the maritime Alps still offer steep climbs such as the one out of the Tinée valley to

Auron, a ski resort less famous, but more attractive, than nearby Isola 2000. From Auron you re-enter the National Park, crossing a landscape that varies from wood- and grassland in the valleys to arid, rocky uplands. Close to the tiny village of Vignols the dolomitic limestone even produces rock towers – a reminder, though on a smaller scale, of the 'real' Dolomites. There are scattered villages too, their conspicuously red-tiled houses clinging to the hillside.

At St Dalmas, west of the famous Mercantour town of St Martin-Vésubie, you are offered one last choice of route. GR52 offers a final chance to enjoy the Mercantour National Park, heading north from St Dalmas and then east before turning south through the Vallée des Merveilles. The marvels of the name are a series of over thirty thousand (perhaps many thousands more) rock engravings. Most date from the Bronze Age, laboriously picked out with an antler. They depict oxen pulling ploughs, daggers, settlements and other, more

THE TOUR DE MONT BLANC

The TMB, a 100 mile (160km) walk involving at least 31,000ft (9,500m) of climbing (depending on the variants chosen), is one of only two walks in the book that are circular, walkers being able to chose their own start point and whether to travel clockwise or anticlockwise. Here we travel anticlockwise, for no better reason than that I have already described the GR5 joining the TMB briefly in that direction, and we start at Le Brévent because it is such a wonderful viewpoint from which to see the Mont Blanc massif and can be easily reached by cable car from Chamonix.

From here the TMB follows GR5 to the Refuge de la Croix du Bonhomme. There is a variation to the TMB from the col above the refuge, heading over the Col de Fours

curious shapes. Most face Mount Bégo. Set where the warm, moist Mediterranean air meets cold, dry alpine air, the mountain sees many thunderstorms and, being ferritic, is often struck by lightning, a fact that suggests that Bronze Age dwellers believed their gods lived in/on the mountain and engraved the rocks for them. To view the engravings it is mandatory to hire a guide, though some pictographs can be seen from the route. This continues through Sospel and on to Menton, bought by France from a cash-strapped Monacan prince, chiefly, it is said, for its lemon orchards. The lemon is celebrated annually in the town in a colourful festival.

The true GR5 heads south, climbing to 6,500ft (2,000m) and staying at that height as it traverses beautiful, rocky country before descending to Utelle, where the chapel of the Madone d'Utelle commemorates a ninth-century miracle. It is said that the sailors of a Spanish ship in danger of being wrecked in a storm off Nice were guided to safety by a miraculous light that lit up the mountain at Utelle. A chapel was built in 880, though the present building dates only from 1806.

The route continues through Levens, a lovely, terraced village, before starting a final descent to Nice. Nice is such a contrast to the remote mountains you have crossed that it seems barely credible that the route through its streets to the Mediterranean is part of the same GR. But there are things to admire here – the old quarter and old port, the museums, even the Promenade des Anglais, despite its roaring traffic and commercialism. Head east along it, avoiding the privatized beaches to find the public area: this is a fine beach for a paddle.

(8,741ft/2,665m) and descending directly to Ville des Glaciers. (From the Tête Nord des Fours, reached by a fifteen-minute walk from Col de Fours, the Matterhorn is visible.) The variation shortens the route, though not appreciably, but is not recommended if snow is still lying or in bad weather, as poor visibility makes route-finding difficult. The 'official' route heads south-east from the refuge on a path that descends steadily, and in places steeply, to Les Chapieux, a village which played unwilling host to the British mountaineer A.W. (Adolphus Warburton) Moore and his guide Christian Almer during the Golden Age of alpinism. Moore is famous for his ascents of the Barre des Écrins (in 1864) in a party that included Edward Whymper and of the Brenva Spur on Mont Blanc (in 1865), and for having accompanied Douglas Freshfield to the Caucasus in 1868. He wrote a delightful book on his climbs (*The Alps in 1864*) in which he described his visit to Les Chapieux, where at the inn he was served a bottle of red wine that was 'perfect vinegar, of the sourest and most undrinkable character'. For this, and an omelette, 'the charge was extortionate', and Moore and Almer were glad to be away from 'such a den of thieves, the situation of which is most dreary and devoid of interest'. You will thankfully find the situation much improved.

The walk now climbs gently up the Vallée des Glaciers, and then more steeply to reach the Italian border at the Col de la Seigne (8,252ft/2,516m), from where there is a marvellous view of the Mont Blanc massif and Val Veni, the next objective. The route through the valley descends to the beautifully sited Refugio Elisabetta Soldini, and then follows an undulating route, with terrific views of the moraine humps of glaciers to the left, and Lac Combal, formed from myriad glacial streams. At the lake there is a variation to the route, the 'official' path taking a high-level route to Courmayeur. The valley route – the preferred option in poor weather – is much easier to follow, using a road and even allowing a bus to be taken from the tiny village of La Visaille to Courmayeur.

Courmayeur is one the best-known Italian ski resorts, but the summer visitor will not be disappointed. From La Palud, north of the town, the Mont Blanc (Monte Bianco) cable car offers one of the best rides in Europe. At the first station, Mont Fréty, is the Giardino Botanico Alpino Saussurea, at 7,127ft/2,173m Europe's highest alpine botanical garden. Named for de Saussure, the garden (open June–September) is well stocked with plants from both the local area and other high places across the world. From Mont Fréty the cable car rises to Pointe Helbronner, and then takes a 3 mile (5km) route above the Glacier de Géant to reach the Aiguille du Midi, from where you can descend to Chamonix.

From Courmayeur the TMB has been recently (2006) rerouted. It no longer follows the ridge of Monte de la Saxe (a stiff climb, though the views are stupendous) but takes a less demanding route north of the ridge to reach Refugio Bonatti (6,633ft/2,022m), named for the great Italian climber Walter Bonatti, whose epic bivouac on the flank of K2 at 26,627ft (8,000m) ensured the success of the 1954 Italian expedition to the world's second highest mountain. Sadly, the aftermath of the 1954 expedition was mired in controversy which lasted for half a century and led to Bonatti's retirement from climbing, though not until after he had produced a series of fine routes, including a solo of the Bonatti Pillar on the Drus.

From the refuge you head for the Swiss border, reaching it at the Grand Col Ferret (8,321ft/2,537m) after a fine walk which descends into Val Ferret before the final climb. Throughout the walk the views are incomparable, both to the west of the great glaciers descending from the Mont Blanc massif, and of Val Ferret itself. From the col, you descend into Switzerland, traversing fine alpine meadow, quintessentially Swiss countryside, in Swiss Val Ferret northwards to Champex, a fine mountain village beside a pleasant lake. The route then continues to Alp Bovine, a dairy farm where the farmer supplements his income serving very welcome refreshments to walkers. In the valley below as the walk continues to the Col de la Forclaz (5,005ft/1,526m) lies the town of Martigny, capital of French-speaking Switzerland and famous for its Roman remains. There is a high-level alternative path to Col de la Forclaz which crosses the high, steep and rugged Fenêtre d'Arpette (8,741ft/2,665m). The route is more in

LEFT Courmayeur.

OPPOSITE
ABOVE Menton, end-point of GR52.
BELOW Walkers can feel out of place among the beautiful people on Promenade des Anglais, Nice, where GR5 reaches the Mediterranean.

keeping with the overall mountain experience of the TMB, but should only be attempted in good weather, when route-finding will be comfortable and the views sensational.

The route reaches the Swiss–French border at the Col de Balme, a notable viewpoint. From here Mont Blanc is visible again; it will be the first time you will have seen the great mountain since the Italian Val Ferret. The next section of the walk is marvellous, following the undulating Posettes ridge before descending to the village of Tré-le-Champ, close to the famous winter sports and climbing centre of Argentière. The next 'official' section of the route involves the use of ladders and other ironmongery to reach the Tête aux Vents. The section offers a bird's-eye view of Argentière but is not for the faint-hearted or those bothered by exposed positions. For those walkers, a variant via the Col de Montets is recommended. A further variant follows, visiting Lac Blanc, one of the most famous viewpoints on the route, where the lake acts as a mirror for the mountain views. Whichever route you choose, the objective is the same: the Chalet de la Flégère at a station on the cable car from Les-Praz-de-Chamonix.

Ahead now is the final stage of the route, in which you traverse a landscape that varies from superb natural scenery to unpleasant sculpturing carried out for the benefit of skiers. The final ascent to Le Brévent requires more ladders and aid, but these should present little difficulty. From the summit you can descend to Chamonix on foot, or by cable car.

ABOVE Autumn, Les Possettes.
LEFT The TMB on the Col de la Forclaz.

THE HAUTE ROUTE

The Haute Route has a long history, having been originally worked out in the last half of the nineteenth century. Then it was a route entirely for mountaineers, as it deliberately chose the highest, occasionally most inaccessible, peaks. In the early years of the last century a ski-tour route was developed. But that, too, required skills that the average walker did not possess and also required a winter (or, at least, early spring) transit that was extremely demanding in terms of equipment and experience. Those issues led, in time, to the development of the Walker's Haute Route. At 110 miles (180km), with about 40,000ft (around 12,000m) of ascent and rising towards the 3,000m (9,840ft) contour, though less exacting than its predecessors the route is still demanding. But with a start and finish at the two most famous peaks of the European Alps, it is also a memorable outing

The walk starts in Chamonix, taking a meandering path to Argentière. From there it follows, more or less, the line of the TMB to Champex, though by way of the variant through the Fenêtre d'Arpette. From Champex it forges its own way, heading north and then east through gentle Swiss countryside and tidy villages to picturesque Le Châble, which sits in the Vallée des Bagne, below its more famous neighbour Verbier. The route now starts in earnest, climbing over 5,000ft (1,600m) to the Cabane du Mont Fort refuge, though the climb can be avoided by taking the cable car to Verbier and on to Les Ruinettes, from where the refuge is a straightforward one-hour walk. Either way, the view is dominated by the Grand Combin (14,150ft/4,314m) to the south.

The route now enters a true mountain wilderness, following the Sentier des Chamois to the Col Termon (8,685ft/2,648m). This route is best avoided in poor weather (ask the guardian at the Mont Fort refuge for advice), when a variant to the Col de Louvie (9,581ft/2,921m) should be taken. Both routes offer wonderful views. Beyond the col, retreat of the Grand Désert Glacier has made progress easier, but the moraine heaps left behind are a sad reminder of global warming. Another high pass, the Col de Prafleuri (9,725ft/2,965m), is reached after a steep climb through country with minimal

The Haute Route shares its route with the TMB from Chamonix to Champex, the two routes enjoying the high peak view from the Col de Balme (BELOW) and of the Glacier du Trient (LEFT).

ABOVE Mont Blanc de Cheilon from near the Refuge de Dix.
LEFT On the Europaweg.

OPPOSITE
The most distinctive peak in the Alps.
The Matterhorn in winter.

waymarking, which makes it trying in poor weather. Beyond the col the Cabane de Prafleuri, built to house workers on the Grand Dixence hydro-electric scheme, is now a luxurious refuge.

The views now improve still further, taking in the Val de Dix with its huge man-made lake (held back by, it is claimed, the world's highest dam wall, at 932ft/284m) and the elegant pyramid of Mont Blanc de Cheilon. The Matterhorn then becomes visible from the amazingly narrow cleft of the Col de Riematten – reached by a steep, difficult path – before the route drops down into the mountain and ski resort of Arolla. From the village the route stays low, taking the Val d'Arolla and the Val d'Hérens, and passing through several lovely Swiss villages, before heading back into the mountains, crossing the Col du Tsaté (9,407ft/2,868m) to reach the foot of the Glacier de Moiry, with its impressive icefall and a refuge at its eastern edge.

Now you head south through the Val de Moiry, the detour to the icefall refuge being avoidable by a variant that leads directly to the Lac de Moiry reservoir. There is then a climb to the Col de Sorebois (9,338ft/2,847m), from where the view of the Weisshorn (14,776ft/4,505m), Zinalrothorn (13,845ft/4,221m) and other peaks south of Zermatt is breathtaking. Avoiding the long descent to Zinal may appeal to many walkers, as the hillside below the cableway is badly scarred and unattractive.

From the now-expanding mountain resort of Zinal the next objective is Gruben in the Turtmann valley. The Haute Route offers several variants. The shortest, and the preferred option for those intent on reaching Zermatt, crosses the Forcletta (9,338ft/2,847m), making its way to the pass across wonderful country and enjoying a fine view from it before dropping down through equally attractive 'soft' country to Gruben, a delightful village. There is one final high pass now, the Augstbordpass at 9,492ft (2,894m), beyond which, at Twära

(8,200ft/2,500m), there is what is deemed by common consent the best viewpoint on the walk. In good weather, the Dom (14,908ft/4,545m), the highest peak wholly within Switzerland, Liskamm (14,849ft/4,527m), Castor (13,868ft/4,228m), Pollux (13,422ft/4,092m) and the Breithorn (13,658ft/4,164m) are all visible.

From Jungen, you can take a cable car to avoid the final descent to St Niklaus, a delightful village clustered around a church with an elaborate clock tower/onion dome/spire. From the village the route reaches Gasenried before following the Europaweg, another of the walk's highlights. The path, which links Grächen, a little north of Gasenried, to Zermatt, is 20 miles (32km) long and was hewn out of the mountains which form the eastern side of the Mattertal in 1997. It is a magnificent mountain walk, with exposed and difficult sections protected by cables, and one 110yd (100m) tunnel which is lit by solar power. The cabling makes sure that walkers are never in any real danger, but there are sections that are occasionally raked with falling stones, particularly after bad weather: these are marked and you are advised to hurry through them as quickly as personal safety allows. You reach the weg by an initial climb of about 2,130ft (650m), but once you are on it the ascent is more gentle, steadily rising to the Europa Hut, where most walkers will spend the night, the whole path being more than can be comfortably managed in a day.

From the hut the way undulates before a final descent into Zermatt. There are few more historically interesting villages in the Alps, and few with a better backdrop. The Matterhorn (14,688ft/4,478m) dominates just about everything in the village, which is no surprise given its classic mountain shape, its isolation and the drama and tragedy associated with its first ascent. Those who wish to know more about that fateful climb, and to see such relics as the rope that broke and so led to the deaths of four men, should head to the Matterhorn Museum.

THE TOUR OF THE MATTERHORN

For many years walking enthusiasts have explored their own way of circumnavigating the Matterhorn, forging a route which made the most of the fine scenery in Switzerland and Italy that surrounds the peak, but only during the present century has a route been formalized. Now, with its own guidebook, this fine 90 mile (145km) walk, involving almost 33,000ft (10,000m) of ascent, is a superb addition to Europe's mountain trails.

It can, of course, be walked in either direction, but the custom is for an anticlockwise path. Starting from Cervinia, this involves climbing to the Theodulpass (10,827ft/3,301m) and descending the Theodulgletscher to Torcknersteg. The glacier is regularly skied, but there are crevasses and sadly accidents occur, so walkers need to exercise extreme caution, and a roped party stands a better chance of a happy descent than an unroped one, particularly if fresh snow is obscuring the surface. From Zermatt, the route reverses the Haute Route to Arolla, returning to Italy at the Col Collon (10,125ft/3,087m). The ascent to the col involves another glacier, so again caution is essential and ropes advisable. The route then crosses the Colle di Valcournera (10,056ft/3,066m), reached by a steep, occasionally cable-aided path, before descending through memorable country to Cervinia.

National Parks and Wildlife

Grouped around Mont Blanc are a series of nature reserves, several of which are traversed by the route. Of special note are the Aiguilles Rouges and Vallon de Berard reserves which, in combination, cover the area from Le Brévent to the valley at Argentière, and are renowned for butterflies, plants and birds.

The Vanoise National Park was created in 1963 and is contiguous with Italy's Gran Paradiso National Park in Italy. The two parks cover an area of 490 sq. miles (1,250 sq. km) and were set up, in large part, to protect the few remaining alpine ibex (*bouquetin* in French), which had been hunted to the edge of extinction. Populations in both parks are now thriving. Other mammals include chamois, marmot and the mountain hare, which turns white in winter. The park is also noted for its alpine plant life, which includes alpine bells, Queen of the Alps and a host of alpine primroses and saxifrages. Bird life includes lammergeier, golden eagle, ptarmigan and black grouse. Similar plants, animals and birds may also be seen in the Queyras Regional Park.

The 268 sq. mile (685 sq. km) Mercantour National Park, created in 1979, has both similar habitats and some that are very different, the proximity of the Mediterranean meaning that in places the park is very Provençal. At altitude you may see chamois and marmot, or even the rarer mouflon. There are also rumoured to be wolves, these having arrived from Italy, though evidence for their existence is very scarce. Lucky high-level walkers may also be entranced by the fabulous lady's slipper orchid or martagon lily, or the attractive, but less exotic, alpine columbine, while at lower elevations you may find olive trees and lavender. Those searching for orchids will likely be rewarded, even if the lady's slipper remains elusive: almost half France's total of about 150 species have been found in the Mercantour.

ABOVE Alpine Ibex.
ABOVE RIGHT Mouflon.
RIGHT Rare butterflies in the Mercantour National Park. Amanda's blue (FAR RIGHT) and Provençal fritillary.

OPPOSITE
LEFT ABOVE Three-veined pink.
LEFT BELOW Reddish stonecrop.
RIGHT Carpathian dog-daisy.

Travel

Walkers on GR5 will have little difficulty in reaching the start or returning from the finish, the airports at both Geneva and Nice being reached by flag-carriers and budget airlines. Chamonix can be reached from Geneva by road in a comfortable hour or so, while both Nice and Zermatt can be reached by train as well as road (though the final section of the journey to the latter has to be by rail).

Maps and guides

The GR5 Trail, Paddy Dillon, Cicerone.
Tour of Mont Blanc, Kev Reynolds, Cicerone.
Chamonix to Zermatt: The Classic Walker's Haute Route, Kev Reynolds, Cicerone.
Tour of the Matterhorn, Hilary Sharp, Cicerone.

The Fédération Française de la Randonnée Pédestre publishes four guides to GR5 which include maps covering the entire route at 1:50,000. However, as usual such strip mapping requires the walker to stay on, or close to, the route as going off the page (as it were) means you are lost. In France the Institut Geographique National (IGN) produces maps at 1:100,000 and at 1:25,000. Four of the larger-scale maps are needed to cover GR5: nos. 45, 53, 54 and 61. Although smaller in scale than the more usual 1:50,000 walking maps, these are adequate when used with the recommended guide. 1:50,000 Série Orange maps are available for those wanting to carry even more mapping. In his guide, Paddy Dillon lists the twenty-one(!) 1:25,000 series maps required for the route, with the novel idea of buying them along the way and posting them home when they become redundant.

TMB: covered by a single IGN 1:50,000 Carte de Randonnées – Pays du Mont-Blanc.

The Haute Route: covered by two 1:50,000 maps from Landeskarte de Suisse (usually known as LS, but with the equivalent French name of Carte Nationale de la Suisse), nos. 5003 and 5006. A full set of 1:25,000 maps is also available.

The Tour of the Matterhorn: two 1:50,000 maps are needed: LS5006 as above, and Istituto Geografico Centrale no. 5. Again, maps at 1:25,000 are available.

Waymarking

GR5 is waymarked with the standard red and white markers. Details of the waymarking of the other routes are given in the recommended guides.

Accommodation

A full range of accommodation is available along the way from mountain refuges and *gîtes d'étape* to small hotels and bed-and-breakfast places in villages, and luxury hotels in Nice and Menton. Carrying camping equipment is useful, as it caters for nothing being available and allows freedom to stop wherever you wish. However, there are restrictions on camping within the National Parks. In France, the pitching of a small tent for one night between the hours of 19.00 and 09.00 is allowed, provided the site is more than one hour's walk from a metalled road.

Equipment

Each of the walks is a high mountain route requiring good equipment, particularly excellent wet weather gear. The mountains can also be cold, so be prepared for chilly weather even in the summer. The glacier crossings of the Tour of the Matterhorn require mountaineering equipment (ice axe, crampons and a rope) even if the weather is good.

Climate

The routes cross country that experiences a typical central European climate. In general this means cold winters and hot summers, but, as usual, mountains influence the climate. Snow will lie on the high passes until early summer, or even much later if there were significant winter falls.

Hazards

The routes are all across high mountain terrain where experience is essential, as an accident that disables a walker can have serious consequences if rescue is delayed, and summoning help may not always be easy. On some sections the walker(s) may encounter few, perhaps no, people. Caution is therefore essential. In poor weather always choose a lower-level variant and be sure to ask at refuges, villages, etc. for advice. There are also sections of each of the walks that use *in situ* cables to aid progress across difficult, exposed terrain. These can present problems for those without sure feet and a head for heights.

OPPOSITE Queen of the Alps.

BELOW Ancient engravings on the rocks below Mont Bégo in the Mercantour National Park. That to the left is believed to represent an ox-team and plough, while that to the right has been given the name *Christos*.

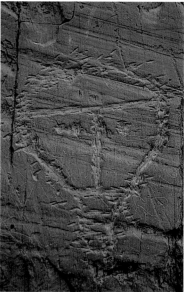

Sentier Martel

VERDON GORGE, FRANCE

For many, Provence is the country of dreams, where in quiet villages you can enjoy an idle breakfast of croissants and coffee during the warm early morning of yet another glorious day. Close by is the coastline of the Côte d'Azur, where beautiful people wander the streets and laze on the beaches of St Tropez, Cannes and Nice. But to the north of the region, up towards the Alps, is a geographical feature for which the region is less well known and indeed was barely known at all until a hundred or so years ago, a feature that is claimed by many to be the most beautiful in Europe. This is the Verdon Gorge, Europe's equivalent of the Grand Canyon (and second in size only to the US canyon).

This gash through the thick Jurassic limestone meanders for over 15 miles (25km) and is, in places, over 2,600ft (700m) deep. For such a depth the gorge is amazingly narrow, only 20ft (6m) wide in places at river level and just 650ft (200m) wide in places at the top. It was carved by the meltwaters of glaciers of the last Ice Age, when, it is estimated, water hammered the existing river valley at a rate exceeding 2,500 tons/sec (about 2,500m³/sec). Entrained rocks added to the scouring effect of the water, cutting the deep channel through which the Verdon River, named for its emerald colour, now flows.

Until 1905 the gorge was unexplored, but that year Édouard-Alfred Martel (1859–1938) travelled down the river, by boat and on foot, on behalf of a French electricity company keen to see if the Verdon might be useful as a source of hydro power. Martel had wanted to be an explorer and initially studied geography at college, but was persuaded to take up law by his parents, who judged that it offered better prospects for wealth and a quiet life than exploration. But Martel's enthusiasm for exploration would not go away, and by 1905 he had become world famous for his discoveries in the huge caves of France's Massif Central, as well as caves elsewhere in Europe, the USA and the Caucasus. In Britain he was the first man to complete the descent of the 345ft (105m) Gaping Gill pothole in Yorkshire in 1895. As well as exploring the cave systems, Martel studied the science of caves, and is now widely regarded as the father of speleology.

Ironically, in view of the enormous risks Martel took in the caves he explored, using equipment and techniques that would chill the blood of a modern caver, he was not keen to complete a full traverse of the Verdon Gorge and had to be persuaded by his team to continue after reaching the Imbut (funnel) which lies west of La Maline. Ultimately

OPPOSITE The Verdon Gorge.

BELOW Cautious walkers on the ladder section near the Brèche Embert.

ABOVE The river is often seen, but rarely reached. When it is, many walkers take the opportunity to rest beside it.

RIGHT A spectacular section of the walk, where the path hugs the base of the cliff on the river's true-right bank.

the team reached Pointe de Galetas, the exit from the gorge. Today five dams have been constructed to harness the power of the river, and one reservoir, the Lac de Ste-Croix, to the west of Galetas, is the largest in France. In 2006 the French government refused Électricité de France permission to pass high-voltage cables through the gorge, a project that would have saved money but ruined the environment.

Within the gorge there are several walking routes, the most famous being the Sentier Martel, named in the great man's honour in 1930. The walk links the French Alpine Club's Chalet de la Maline to Pointe Sublime, passing through the most spectacular section of the gorge and

forming part of the GR4 long-distance footpath. From the chalet you descend 1,150ft (350m) to the river along a path that zigzags down wooded cliffs. Further on is the Pré d'Issane, a small pebble beach where many walkers take a moment to cool their feet in the river. Beyond, the gorge narrows at the Étroit des Cavaliers and then crosses scree to reach a possible detour. Close by, the Artuby River reaches the Verdon at a sharp horseshoe bend, and you can reach the viewpoint of La Mescla by an out-and-back detour.

Back on the Sentier Martel, the path climbs to overcome the finger of rock which forms the horseshoe bend, descending the series of stairways (with a total of over 250 stairs) of the Brèche Embert. A fine section of gorge walking now takes you below several belvederes on the road that follows the upper edge of the gorge closely. At these viewpoints, visitors can watch rock climbers in action on the vast, sheer walls, or peer into the depths of the gorge, but for walkers the view is much more restricted. You pass another pebble beach, and the Tours de Trescaïre, two huge rock towers across the river, before traversing three tunnels, originally bored to aid hydro-electric projects but long abandoned. Torches are handy here, though it is possible to make do without if you take care. The tunnels are also surprisingly cool, even on the warmest of days. Beyond the second tunnel (Tunnel de Trescaïre) there is a fine view of the narrow gorge, while in the final tunnel (Tunnel du Baou) an excavated exit allows you to reach the Baume aux Pigeons and a view of the tight Couloir Samson (Samson's Corridor). Exiting from the last tunnel you reach Pointe Sublime, a famous viewpoint where you can enjoy one last look along the gorge before having to solve the problem of returning to a car parked near La Maline. The simplest way is to hitch-hike: many of the visitors at Sublime head along the gorge crest road and are very willing to offer a lift.

Walk information

Map: IGN Serie Bleue (1:25,000), sheet 3442Est. Start: Chalet de la Maline: Finish: Pointe Sublime. Length: 9½ miles (15km). Ascent: 500ft (150m), but 1,650ft (500m) of descent. Please note: there are no exits along the walk and on hot days Sentier Martel can be very tiring.

The view of the gorge from the Baume aux Pigeons.

The Jungfrau Horseshoe

SWITZERLAND

Many years ago I worked as a glaciologist at the Jungfraujoch, a research station that was a surprise to most day trippers, who had no idea that there was anything except a tourist station at the *joch* (pass), and that people worked and lived there, enjoying a wondrous peace and solitude when the last train of the day disappeared. My work was on the Aletsch Glacier, the longest glacier, and the largest by area, in the European Alps (and, since 2001, part of a UNESCO World Heritage Site). Living for long periods at 11,316ft (3,450m) meant excellent acclimatization, and this, and the ability to start out early before the first train had deposited to the day's climbers, allowed me to make rapid and comfortable ascents of the Jungfrau and evening climbs of the Mönch.

At weekends away from the station my colleagues and I linked paths to form a circular walk. The start had to be Wilderswil: take the train to Schynige Platte and walk to the First lift. Then across to Grosse Scheidegg. Bypass Grindelwald, staying close to the Wetterhorn and climbing towards Kleine Scheidegg. Head west to the Lauterbrunnen valley and climb to the magnificent viewpoint of Piz Gloria. Then descend, perhaps through Mürren, or directly to Wilderswil. The rack railway which linked most of these places was always there to aid a quick exit if time was short or the weather bad.

When preparing this book I discovered that this route – its exact course is routinely argued over, in good-natured fashion, by the glaciologists of several nations – is now formalized and has its own guidebook. And so it should. It is a marvellous route, about 70 miles (115km), with 21,300ft (6,500m) of climbing, visiting the best viewpoints of the Bernese Oberland's most famous peaks, and linking them in fine style.

The route starts in Wilderswil, where a fine nineteenth-century church can be reached by crossing the ancient covered bridge over the Lütschine River. Close to the village are the romantic ruins of the nineteenth-century Unspunnen Castle. By tradition the castle was the home of Manfred in Byron's Gothic poem of that name, written, it is thought, as a result of the famous 'ghost-story' sessions at Geneva which were also the impetus for Mary Shelley's Frankenstein. Today the ruins are the centre for an annual festival of local culture with traditional costumes and dances, and strong men attempting to throw the Unspunnen stone furthest.

Early on the walk from Schynige Platte to First the route passes areas of limestone pavement which are excellent for alpine flowers and butterflies.

From Wilderswil a path tackles the 4,500ft (1,400m) climb to Schynige Platte, but it is rarely walked: in this area of the Bernese Oberland railways are part of the landscape and should be enjoyed, not dismissed. Opened in 1893, the cog railway takes forty-five minutes to reach the real start of the route (and the Alpine Garden – see below). The walk starts by following the Faulhornweg, one of the finest day walks in the Alps, though an early option along the Panoramaweg has considerable merit: you walk beside the Alpine Garden, take a narrow ridge in a superb position to reach a ladder below the Loucherhorn and then descend to rejoin the Faulhornweg. The Faulhornweg leads through increasingly rocky country to the Weber Hut (or Berghütte Männdlenen, to give it its proper title), where food and drink are available.

A long climb now takes you towards the Faulhorn. It is not necessary to reach the summit, though most walkers will want to, enjoying not only the view from the oldest mountain hotel in Switzerland (built in 1830) which sits on the summit but the possibility of further refreshment. From the summit, the route descends to the northern shore of the Bachsee and, if weather permits, one of the classic views of the Alps, the Oberland peaks reflected in its waters. Beyond, the walk follows a wide, easy path to the top station of the First ski lift. Originally a double chair lift – a very long chair lift (the longest in Europe), for which old and heavy coats were wrapped around skiers to keep out the chill of the ride – the First lift now has small, modern gondolas which take visitors to Grindelwald, a delightful town, in comfort.

From the lift station the walk takes a gently undulating path through high alpine meadow to the pass at Grosse Scheidegg, where the Berghotel has accommodation for over a hundred people and an excellent restaurant. The hotel sits on a pass between the Rosenlauital, heading down to Meiringen, and the Grindelwald valley, a marvellous viewpoint. A road crosses the pass, but traffic is restricted to buses. In winter the road is a favourite toboggan run for skiers having a day off from the pistes. The walk descends with the road, crossing it, using it and staying close to it all the way to the classical alpine chalet of the Hotel Wetterhorn, named for the mountain that stands above it. The peak (at 12,110ft/3,692m one of the lowest local tops, but because of its bulk and position one which dominates the area) was first climbed in 1844, but its ascent in 1854 by the English mountaineer Sir Alfred Wills is now considered to have been the first climb of the Golden Age of alpine mountaineering. Winston Churchill climbed the peak in 1894. A plaque on an old gondola close to the hotel is a reminder of the plan, in 1908, to take a cable car to the Wetterhorn's summit. The still-visible ruins of a mid-station, to which cars ran until 1915, are all that remain of this ambitious venture.

From the hotel, a wooden staircase (with about nine hundred steps: there is a fee for the ascent) leads to a view of the now fast-retreating Oberer (Upper) Grindelwald Glacier and the gorge of its meltwater stream. Our journey, though, follows a forest track that climbs past another restaurant to reach open country and the top of the Pfingstegg cable car from Grindelwald. The cable car is popular with visitors, who use it to follow a path our route also takes. However, the visitors usually aim for the Unterer (Lower) Grindelwald Glacier, bearing left off the walking route. Until 2005 there was a very popular restaurant

From the walk there are occasional glimpses of Brienzersee and a fine view of Sägistalsee in the mountain hollow below the Schmabhorn.

ABOVE Looking back towards Schynige Platte from the foot of the Sägistal valley.

LEFT The Männdlenen (or Weber) Hut is a useful refreshment stop before the long climb to the Faulhorn.

in the mountain amphitheatre filled by the glacier, but in that year the collapse of half a million tons of moraine destroyed it, as well as altering the landscape. The collapse resulted from glacier shrinkage, after which ice no longer held the rock debris in place. There are concerns that further collapses might occur, and notices warn walkers to beware of falling rocks.

Our route ignores the glacier path – though a detour that way is worthwhile if time permits – crossing the gorge of the outflowing stream from the glacier and then climbing, occasionally steeply and aided by engineered steps, to Boneren, a log cabin at 4,946ft (1,508m). More gradual climbing and then it reaches a col at 5,740ft (1,750m) before descending to Alpiglen (5,314ft/1,620m), famous as the start point for many climbers attempting the north face of the Eiger.

The Eiger's north face remains the most notorious mountain wall in Europe among non-climbers, in large part because of eight men having died attempting it before the first successful ascent in 1938 by a four-man team (Heckmair, Vörg, Kasparek and Harrer, the latter famous as the author of *Seven Years in Tibet* and *The White Spider*, the latter a history of early attempts and ascents of the wall). The similarity in German between Nordwand (north wall) and Mordwand (death wall) aided headline writers, and even after many successful climbs, the wall has maintained its reputation, one reinforced by the deaths that still occur.

The Eiger is limestone, and annual freezing and thawing loosens the rock, adding stone fall to the hazard of the peak's position, which attracts bad weather. The wall's position – it rears up from alpine meadows close to Kleine Scheidegg – also means that dramas on it are played out to an audience watching through high-power telescopes, which does not happen on other climbs. In 1966 during the first ascent of a direct route up the face, the American John Harlin fell to his death when a rope broke, his fall witnessed by those watching. Today, the White Spider, a many-armed ice sheet high up towards the summit made famous because of Harrer's book, is shrinking back as the earth warms: its disappearance will be sad – the loss of a mountaineering icon.

From Alpiglen the route traces a path across the scree and alpine pasture at the foot of the Eiger's north face, though foreshortening means that the wall is somewhat less imposing from here than when viewed from the station on the Jungfraujoch railway, where a tunnel has been bored through the mountain so that visitors can peer out and the true angle is apparent. The route follows the path as it leaves the north wall, climbing to the Eiger's west ridge and the Eigergletscher station, where accommodation is available.

Looking back down the climb up towards the Faulhorn.

ABOVE The high peaks of the Horseshoe from below the Faulhorn's summit. To the left is the Eiger, with the Mönch behind and to the right. Next right is the Jungfrau.

LEFT The north face of the Eiger in winter. The photograph was taken from the Mannlichen, above Kleine Scheidegg.

The Shreckhorn beyond the Bachsee. Such wonderfully clear days make the walk from Schynige Platte one of the finest outings in the Alps.

Eigergletscher, named for the glacier that flows down the Eiger's south-western face, is the station that precedes the section of the Jungfraujoch railway that goes through the peak. The railway is an engineering masterpiece, begun in 1896 but not completed until 1912 because of the difficulty of tunnelling through the mountain. The line follows a rising semicircle, with tunnels cut to the outside world both on the north wall and at Eismeer, where the view is into the amphitheatre below the northern flank of the Fiescherhorn.

At Eigergletscher you can descend to Kleine Scheidegg, where refreshments, souvenirs, the railway and the north wall telescope can all be found. The hamlet – little more than the station, hotel, shop and restaurant – stands on a pass, the name, which means 'little watershed', indicating the fact that the pass splits the upper valley of the Lütschine River into two: one arm of the river, the Weisse Lütschine (white Lütschine), flows through the Lauterbrunnen valley, while the other, the Schwarze Lütschine (black Lütschine), flows past Grindelwald. (The two arms meet close to the aptly named village of Zweilütschinen.) Interestingly, the 'little watershed' of Kleine Scheidegg is, at 6,760ft (2,061m), higher than the 'big watershed' of Grosse Scheidegg, the latter's name reflecting its more important position, a pass separating the Lütschine and Reichenbach valleys. The Reichenbach valley, as all readers of Conan Doyle's books will know, is home to the falls where Sherlock Holmes apparently dies when he and Moriarty fall during a final fight. Close to the summit of the Lauberhorn, which rises above Kleine Scheidegg to the south-west, is the start of the one of the classic races of the annual downhill ski calendar. To regain the route from Kleine Scheidegg, return to Eigergletscher.

You head eastwards along a moraine crest of the Eiger Glacier, and then descend through forest and farmland, passing Biglenalp and Mettla to reach Prechalp, where snacks and drinks are available. The descent steepens now, engineered paths, a ladder and fixed wire ropes aiding progress. Be careful here, as the ground can be treacherous if damp. The bonus is the Trummelbach Gorge, carved by the stream of that name as it plummets into the Lauterbrunnen valley. The most attractive section of the steep gorge carved by the plunging stream can be accessed from the valley floor, where you can pay an entrance fee to view illuminated waterfalls within the mountain.

Lauterbrunnen means 'having many fountains', the valley being named for the waterfalls that pour over the huge, sheer valley walls. The most famous is the Staubbach, which inspired Goethe to write *Gesang der Geister über den Wassern* (The Song of the Spirits of the Waters). This lies to the north of the route's entry into the valley, but you will pass smaller, though impressive falls near Stechelberg, which lies at the end of the valley road.

The next objective is the Schilthorn, which can be reached by a path that heads directly up the Sefinental. In his guide to the route, Kev Reynolds recommends a more alpine approach to this valley than the easy path beside the Sefinen Lütschine, heading for Obersteinberg, a route which passes a fine hostelry, Berghaus Trachsellauenen, and the Hotel Tschingelhorn before reaching Berghotel Obersteinberg. His route is a fine walk, but involves over 2,600ft (800m) of climbing, and further climbing before a descent can be made into the Sefinental. Once you are in the valley, there is more climbing, from the valley floor to the Rostock Hut (6,688ft/2,039m – accommodation for about fifty people and an excellent restaurant) and on to the Schilthorn

LEFT Viewed head-on as it is approached during the walk, the Wetterhorn is a much less shapely peak than when viewed from Grindelwald or from the the top of the First ski lift (BELOW).

OPPOSITE The Eiger, too, looks very different when viewed from an oblique angle. From Kleine Scheidegg it gives the impression of being bulky, but viewed as here, from Grosse Scheidegg, the north-east (Mittellegi) ridge is razor-sharp, the whole peak appearing much more delicate.

ABOVE The Aletsch Glacier. The glacier is the longest, and has the largest surface area, of any glacier in Europe (outside of Iceland). It forms part of the Jungfrau-Aletsch Protected Area, which was declared a UNESCO World Heritage Site in 2001. The glacier is reached from Kleine Scheidegg by a rack railway which runs inside the Eiger.

OPPOSITE
ABOVE Alpenglow on the north face of the Eiger.
BELOW LEFT Grindelwald from the path near the Upper Grindelwald Glacier.
BELOW RIGHT Kleine Scheidegg.

(9,742ft/2,970m). The walking is not easy: this is the hardest part of the entire route and in bad weather should not be attempted, as in its early stages the path is not always readily discernible and so good visibility is needed to spot landmarks. The upper section of the route is also exposed, with wire ropes and fixed ladders to aid progress. The first part of the walk climbs to the pass of Rote Härd, from where an exposed, occasionally aided, route follows a narrow ridge to the cable car station.

The Schilthorn is topped by the revolving Piz Gloria restaurant. The 400-seater restaurant was in the process of construction when the makers of the James Bond film *On Her Majesty's Secret Service* chose it as the major location. The film company contributed to the final construction. Blofeld, the film's villain, had a mountaintop lair called Piz Gloria, and the name was transferred to the restaurant. The 40ft (12m) diameter rotating core turns one full revolution each hour. Though most famous for the Bond film, the Schilthorn is also well known to skiers as the start of the Inferno downhill ski race, first run in January 1928 at the behest of Sir Arnold Lunn, the ski race pioneer. Originally the race had a mass start and finished in Mürren, a drop of 4,360ft (1,330m) over a horizontal distance of about 3.75 miles (6km). The first winner took 1 hour 12 minutes to reach Mürren: Sir Arnold finished sixth. Today the race is run on a prepared piste from the summit to Mürren, and then on natural snow to Lauterbrunnen.

From the summit the view to the three great peaks of the northern wall of the Bernese Oberland is superb. The peak names are said to derive from an old legend of a young girl (Jungfrau) being protected from the clutches of an ogre (Eiger) by a monk (Mönch). However, as

ABOVE Having dropped into the Lauterbrunnen valley the route heads up the Sefinental, then takes the ridge at the centre of the photograph to reach the Rote Hard, the low point on the ridge, to the right, and the Schilthorn.

LEFT Warning sign at the Schilthorn. All the paths from the top require rather better footwear.

ABOVE Mürren.
BELOW LEFT Decorated fire hydrant, Mürren.

is often the case, the real reason might be more prosaic: the Eiger could be named from *acer*, sharp, or *ger*, a spear, because of the sharpness of the Mittellegi Ridge or the resemblance of the triangular north face to an spear tip. Then, if land below the Mönch was owned by monks – not an unusual occurrence in medieval Europe – the Jungfrau might have been named to fit the legend inspired by the other two names.

From the Schilthorn the route descends over difficult scree, occasionally aided by wire ropes – look out for the memorial to a young Englishwoman, Alice Arbuthnot, killed by lightning in 1865 while on her honeymoon – and then bears right on a path for Schiltalp, passing the delightful Grauseeli Lake. Next it descends more steeply, with occasional aided sections, to reach Schiltalp (6,389ft/1,948m – snacks and drinks). It is now possible to bypass Mürren, but who would want to? This is a lovely little village, vehicle-free (more or less), and with a collection of window-boxed wooden chalets. A true delight. Look out for the memorial to Sir Alfred Lunn, who put the village on the winter tourist map when, as the memorial notes, he set the first slalom course in 1922 and organized the first official races in 1931. Add in the Inferno, and Mürren owes much to Lunn.

If you avoid Mürren, the route passes two *pensions*, Suppenalp and Sonnenberg, each offering accommodation and meals. From the latter the route crosses farmland to reach the lush, dairy-farm valley of Soustal. Beyond is the side valley of the Suls stream and the Swiss Alpine Club's Lobhornhütte, which has accommodation for about twenty-five people and an excellent restaurant. Now it remains only to descend through more rich farmland, though crossing the Sylertal requires great care, particularly if winter snow is still lying, as the valley is steep and shadowed, the combination occasionally creating icy conditions. Continue through Saxeten, and then make the final descent to Wilderswil.

THE ALPINE PASS ROUTE

While researching for this book I cam across another guide by the thoroughly excellent Kev Reynolds, one to the Alpine Pass route (also published by Cicerone), a 206 mile (330km) traverse of Switzerland that takes in almost all the country's major alpine passes, and involves 59,000ft (18,000m) of climbing as a result. Linking Sargans and Montreux, the route uses, in its central section, part of the Bernese Oberland Horseshoe and has the potential to become as popular as the HRP of the Pyrénées (see page 28).

ABOVE Les Diablerets, above Gsteig. Crossing the range is one of the highlights of the Alpine Pass route.

OPPOSITE Yellow mountain saxifrage.

Travel

By air The closest airport is at Bern. The alternative is a road or rail journey after a flight to Zurich or Geneva.

By rail Main lines link all Switzerland's main cities to Interlaken, from where the mountain railway goes to Grindelwald, Lauterbrunnen, Kleine Scheidegg and Wengen.

By road The Swiss motorway and main road system provides an efficient way of reaching Interlaken and the mountain railway. It is also possible to drive to Grindelwald and follow the Lauterbrunnen valley as far as Stechelberg.

Maps and guides

Tour of the Jungfrau Region, Kev Reynolds, Cicerone.

An excellent guide to the horseshoe walk by a doyen of UK guide writers.

Bundesamt für Landestopographie (the official Swiss mapmakers) cover the route with two 1:50,000 Wanderkarte sheets, nos. 254T (Interlaken) and 264T (Jungfrau). The same company also produces 1:25,000 maps. Three are required: sheets 1229, 1248 and 1268.

Waymarking

The Swiss walking signs are among the best in Europe, marking not only destinations but also probable walking times. The horseshoe route does not have a specific designation, but you are unlikely to get lost (though map and guide, as always, are essential).

Accommodation

Because the route stays reasonably close to villages and to the mountain railway, it is possible to complete the walk in fine style, staying in the better hotels in Grindelwald, Kleine Scheidegg and the Lauterbrunnen valley (and even in Wengen). Hotels at the lower end of the scale can also be used, but these are rather more difficult to find outside Grindelwald. The route also passes several mountain huts. There are many good campsites in the area. Technically wild camping is not allowed, but it is usually possible to persuade a local landowner to let you stay one night. Beyond the last farmed land one night's discreet camping (i.e. pitch late, leave early, don't leave the tent up all day) will probably be OK.

Equipment

The equipment required depends on the accommodation to be used. In summer, in good weather, a day sac, good boots and lightweight gear is all you will need. However, though the area has a large number of well-marked walking paths, so escape from genuinely foul weather is usually not a problem, as with all mountain areas it would be foolish to set off without windproof and wet weather gear.

Climate

As the first big mountain range encountered by any weather heading south, the Bernese Oberland in general, and the Eiger in particular, is notorious for generating bad weather. Spring, summer and autumn can all have periods of settled weather which allow wonderful walking, though winter snow may make the higher sections of the route tricky in spring and early snowfalls can hamper progress in autumn.

Hazards

None really. The abundance of alternative routes and proximity of both villages and the railway make this a safe route. That said, the usual walking hazards – sprained ankle etc. – can turn a benign day in the hills into a misery.

Wildlife

The Bernese Oberland is not part of a National Park, but the pastoral nature of much of the country it crosses and wild mountain fringes of the route mean that you may well see something unusual. The plant lover will be looking out for Edelweiss and the beautiful pink alpine rose, and may also see alpine snowbell, alpine and spring pasque flowers, willow-leaved gentian and several different orchids. The Alpine Garden, close to the top station of the Schynige Platte railway at the start of the walk, claims to have specimens of over 90 per cent of Switzerland's flowers.

You will need to be lucky to see many mammals, though you may see chamois and alpine ibex and very occasionally glimpse mouflon.

The marmot is much more likely to be seen, though here as elsewhere you will need patience to see, rather than just hear the whistle of, this rodent.

In the forested areas of the walk the lucky walker may see or hear the nutcracker. Alpine choughs are much more likely to be observed, particularly if you head for the Jungfraujoch, or choose to share a picnic with the birds. For the bird lover, an interesting place to visit is the Alpine Bird Park near Ischboden, close to the route below Grosse Scheidegg, where injured birds are nursed back to health; here local species can be observed at close quarters.

RIGHT ABOVE Snow gentian.
RIGHT BELOW Field gentian.
BELOW Alpine marmot.

OPPOSITE
LEFT ABOVE Willow-leaved gentian.
LEFT BELOW Purple gentian.
RIGHT ABOVE Chalkhill blue on plume knapweed.
RIGHT CENTRE Apollo on Rhaetian knapweed.
RIGHT BELOW Painted lady on thorny thistle.

Klettersteig Mürren

BERNESE OBERLAND, SWITZERLAND

A 'best day walk' in Switzerland might be the walk from Schynige Platte to First, part of the Bernese Oberland tour on page 94; it could also be another distinctly different outing. The use of *vie ferrate* – iron roads created by soldiers of the First World War to reach and fight on alpine ridges (see page 158), suitably refined by modern equipment and safety considerations – provides the non-climber with sure feet and a head for heights with the opportunity to reach otherwise impossibly difficult places, and to enjoy the sensation of exposure in a safe, controlled way. One such *via ferrata*, in German a *klettersteig*, has recently been opened close to Mürren. It differs from the standard route in being horizontal rather than vertical, exploring the western wall of the Lauterbrunnen valley and offering terrific views and one or two sensational positions. The route is long (about 2 miles/3km, but it feels longer), several hours being needed for a traverse.

Please note: to accomplish this route, as with all *vie ferrate*, specialized equipment and the ability to use it safely are absolutely essential. You MUST have a climbing harness equipped with a *vie ferrate* kit comprising two long slings attached to the harness, each ending with a karabiner which clips to the guide/safety wire on the route. Where the wire is anchored to the rock face, unclip the lead karabiner and reattach it to the wire beyond the anchor. Then move the second karabiner. At NO TIME must you be unattached to the wire: one karabiner MUST ALWAYS be attached. Helmets are essential in case of stone fall from above and because, occasionally, steep rock may mean your head hits the rock face as you move up. Good, treaded boots are essential, particularly in damp conditions, as metal rungs can be slippery. Gloves are handy, as the wires can make hands sore after prolonged climbing.

In its early stages, the *klettersteig* is straightforward, the drops into the Lauterbrunnen valley shielded by vegetation (OPPOSITE), but later the walker/climber is faced with more demanding exposure (RIGHT).

LEFT The most exposed section of the route. Here there is nothing to hide the exposure, and the drop into the valley is both sheer and enormous.

BELOW Twice along the way the walker/climber must negotiate a single, thin wire. a test of concentration as well as nerve. This is the most dramatic of the two sections, with a roaring waterfall to the right and a drop of several hundred metres below.

OPPOSITE The dramatic-looking, but relatively straightforward, 'Nepal bridge'. Once across, there are only a few metres of the route to go. The cable car from Stechelberg, in the valley, to Gimmelwald passes close to the bridge (off to the left in this photograph) giving travellers in the gondola an awe-inspiring view of the bridge.

The route starts in Mürren's lower village at the Sportchalet (not to be confused with the Sportzentrum in the upper village) where you go into the tunnel on the south side of the wall of the tennis courts, exiting on to a grassy field. The wires start to the left here, going across the masonry wall. Once you have put on the full equipment, you can start off along the wall path. The route soon descends slightly and starts the traverse of the valley wall, though the position is not exposed. The view expands, north-east to the Eiger's steep profile, south towards the valley end. Next comes the most exposed section of the route. It is short, but the drop – about 2,000ft (600m) or so to the valley floor – can be unnerving. Do not rush: take time to ensure you have clipped and unclipped correctly and you will be safe.

The route is only open from mid-June to October, and during that time guides can be hired to accompany those new to *via ferrata*. Guides are essential for the Tyrolean traverse you reach beyond the exposed section, where you are drawn across a bottomless chasm on a rope. Those without guides bypass the traverse by using a single rope bridge. As this crosses the same chasm, but with the accompaniment of a roaring waterfall, and requires sure-footedness, it is not the easy option.

Further on you reach another, shorter rope bridge, and a series of ladders which descend the sheer valley wall (though the exposure here is not great). Next a rising traverse through woodland allows a view of the cable car station at Gimmelwald, the terminus of the route. But there is one final obstacle to be overcome, a long 'Nepal bridge' over another yawning chasm. Illustrations of the bridge suggest that several walkers can use it at once, but it is not as stable as it appears, and the more traffic, the greater the swing, so first timers should traverse one at a time. When finally on solid ground and freed of the need to clip into a wire, head off into the village for a celebratory drink: if this was your first *via ferrata* you have deserved it.

Walk information

Map: Not essential – just follow the wire – but to sort out the view along the way Landeskarte der Schweiz 1:50,000 sheet 264T is useful. Start: Mürren. Finish: Gimmelwald. If you use the cable cars to reach the start and return from the finish, then the valley car park near the base station near Stechelberg is a good start point. Length: 2 miles (3km). Ascent: about 300ft (100m).

Via Alpina

GERMANY

In 1971 L'association Grande Traversée des Alpes was formed in France with the intention of integrating long-distance footpaths across the eight Alpine nations of Europe – Austria, France, Germany, Italy, Liechtenstein, Monaco, Slovenia and Switzerland. The proposal suggested that such a venture would offer an additional way of promoting tourism to the Alps by offering new opportunities for local guides and accommodation; and it would be in harmony with the idea of sustainable development of the mountain environment. However, not until 1991 and the signing of the Alpine Convention by the Alpine nations was the idea of a unified cross-Alp route – the Via Alpina – able to really take shape. It did so with the waymarking of the Red Trail from Trieste, at the Italian–Slovenian border, through all eight Alpine nations to finish in Monaco, a distance of 1,600 miles (2,400km) in 161 linked stages. The route crosses national borders 44 times.

The Red Trail was followed by a further four trails – Blue, Green, Purple and Yellow – which offered the chance to explore sections of the Alps. Each is less ambitious than the Red Trail, varying from the 13 stages of the Green Trail in Liechtenstein and Switzerland to the 66 stages of the Purple Trail, which explores the Julian Alps, Austria's mountains and the Bavarian Alps.

Every walker will have favourite sections among the vast mileage of the various trails. Here I explore the two routes through Germany's Bavarian Alps, with a slight emphasis on the Red Trail which, though shorter, traverses marvellous mountain scenery close to the Austria–Germany border.

THE PURPLE TRAIL

The trail enters Germany from Austria as it crosses the Steinernen Meer (Stone Sea), a high limestone plateau to the south of Berchtesgaden. The plateau is a famous example of karst, a landscape where underground streams carve out passages and caves that make the area the most important in Germany for speleologists.

Beyond the Stone Sea, with its isolated clumps of small pines, the route descends to the Karlingerhaus, one of the most beautifully positioned of all alpine huts, set in a mountain hollow beside the Funtensee; then it descends again into the Berchtesgaden National Park. Inevitably the Berchtesgaden Alps, which form a centrepiece of the National Park, are as famous for their Nazi connections as their mountain scenery and wildlife. The Kehlsteinhaus (nicknamed the Eagle's Nest by a French diplomat) still attracts many visitors, most of

whom do not realize that it was built as a teahouse, a fiftieth birthday present for Adolf Hitler in 1939, and was not a Reich headquarters. The actual headquarters were situated at the foot of the mountain, at Obersalzberg: the buildings there have now all been demolished.

After descending past the excellent Schrainbach Waterfall the route reaches St Bartholomä on the western shore of the Königsee. The latter name is usually translated King's Lake, though many experts believe this to be incorrect, preferring Kuno's Lake, Kuno being a popular local Christian name. The village is named for the patron saint of farmers; the church in his honour is a marvellous onion-domed construction. West of the village rises the east face of the Watzmann which, at 5,900ft (1,800m), is the tallest mountain wall in the eastern Alps. The face is a hard climb, but one that attracts many climbers, over a hundred of whom have died attempting it. Perhaps the most famous of those who succeeded was Hermann Buhl, the legendary Austrian climber who climbed the face at night in midwinter as a prelude to the 1953 Nanga Parbat expedition. Depending on the definition of an independent mountain, as opposed to a subsidiary peak on an extended ridge, the Watzmann is the second, third or fourth highest peak in Germany.

The next section of the route is the easiest, as well as among the most interesting, as it involves travelling to the northern end of the Königsee by ferry, a relaxing voyage through stunning scenery. You disembark at Königsee village and head east through alpine meadow and upland forest along the spine of the peaks that form the northern boundary of the National Park. The section of the trail to the Neue Traunsteiner Hut follows, in part, the route of an old brine pipeline. The local area, including Bad Reichenhall, to the north, and Salzburg (salt town), to the east in Austria, were famous for the production of salt, some mines still being open to visitors. One of the easiest ways of transporting the salt from source was to dissolve it and allow the brine to flow downhill in pipes. Ramsau, which the route brushes past, was a centre for the inhalation of brine steam as a cure for chest problems.

The Purple Trail now crosses into Austria, returning to Bavaria to head north to Ruhpolding, a pleasant village that was once a spa resort but is now more famous for its biathlon circuit, which has been home to several World Cup events, most recently in 2009. On again, the trail heads west on an undulating route through the Chiemgau Alps which rise between the Rivers Inn and Saalach. Here the high points offer marvellous views, the very best being from Hochfelln,

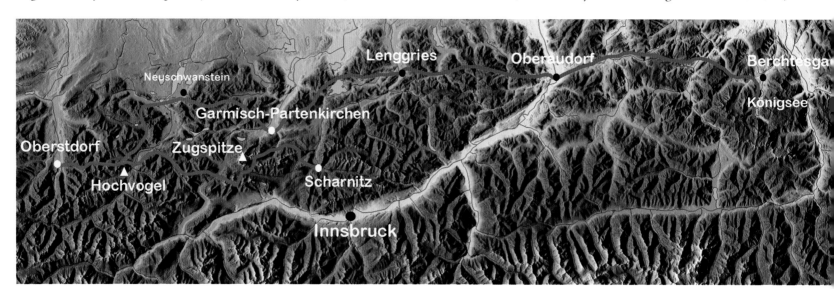

ABOVE St Bartholomä, with the Watzmann rising behind it.
RIGHT Lucky travellers on the Königsee ferry will have the guide who uses a trumpet (which he plays extremely well) to illustrate the amazing echo from the cliffs at the northern end of the lake.

The fairy-tale castle of Neuschwanstein. The castle is open to visitors daily 9am-6pm (10am-4pm from October to March). Tel: 08362 930830.

(5,474ft/1,669m), which is accessible by Germany's second longest cable car from the village of Bergen, ensuring you will not be alone. On the next stage you could be forgiven for using the Hochplatte chair lift, though this cuts out only the first stage of the climb to Hochplatte. There follows a terrific ridge traverse to the jagged Kampenwand (5,474ft/1,669m), the summit of which is reached by a scramble that requires a good head for heights (though the route actually bypasses the top). The descent from the summit has its moments too, a wire rope aiding progress to Steinling Alm before a superb section of undulating ridge walking, with fine alpine meadows and glorious views, reaches a descent through Austria to the Inn valley. Here you cross the river (which doubles as the national border) and the Munich–Innsbruck motorway to reach Oberaudorf.

To the west of the Inn is a group of relatively low peaks usually named for the prominent lakes, the Tegernsee and Schliersee, which lie at their northern fringe. The peaks offer easy walking through alpine meadows and woodland, with only moderate climbing to a series of fine viewpoints. It is claimed that from the summit chapel of Seeon Alm (4,536ft/1,383m), a slight detour from the route, 200 named peaks are visible. You continue through larch forest, over Traithen (1,852m), descend, and then climb to the Rotwandhaus refuge (5,789ft/1,765m). You need to take care on the trail in this area, but the views are sensational: both the Berchtesgaden and Allgäu Alps are visible – the first and last blocks of the Bavarian Alps to be climbed along the Purple route.

The mountain railway to Taubenstein allows a speedy descent to the Spitzingsee, a lovely, forest-shrouded lake which is the centrepiece of an important winter sports area. The walking is easier now, through alpine meadow with one last climb before a descent to Sutten. Beyond,

ABOVE Garmisch-Partenkirchen in midwinter, from the summit of the Zugspitze. The Purple Trail drops down into the town from the Estergebirge (top right of the photograph), then climbs Kramerspitze, to the left.
RIGHT The famous ski jumps at Garmisch-Partenkirchen.

The Red Trail reaches Germany at Scarnitz, from where it follows the Satteltal, a valley which heads towards Gehrenspitze (to the right). It then goes north, passing behind the Dreitorspitze (to the left) to reach the Reintal.

there is fine woodland walking until the rather more demanding climb to Risserkogel (5,989ft/1,826m). From the summit there is a marvellous view north to Tegernsee, usually enhanced by the hang gliders who regularly use the nearby peak of Wallberg, easily reached on the Wallbergbahn. You descend along woodland paths to Kreuth, a tiny village famous for the spring of healing water which bubbles up a short distance to the south at Wildbad Kreuth. Legend has it that the spring was discovered by a hunter who had wounded a deer and, after following it, discovered the animal using spring water to bathe its wounds. It would be good to report that the hunter spared the deer in thanks for the find, but the fate of the animal is not recorded.

There is more woodland walking, but with occasional fine views heading west to Lenggries, which has an interesting private museum of local natural history. Those interested in the local wildlife will enjoy both it and the next stage of the walk, as the Benediktenwand cliffs are now home to alpine ibex (steinbock), which have become relatively tame and so allow a reasonably close approach. Those not keen on exposed terrain will be less thrilled, as the cliff section requires a sure foot and a head for heights. Although the walking into Garmisch-Partenkirchen is now straightforward and, usually, through alpine meadow, there are further exposed sections on the descent into the Loisachtal valley, some of them with chains to aid progress.

Garmisch and Partenkirchen were two towns until 1935, when Hitler forced the mayors to accept combining in the run-up to the Winter Olympics of 1936. Today most Germans and visitors refer to the combined town as Garmisch, to the aggravation of the population

Zugspitze from Gribigstein. To see this view of Germany's highest peak (the summit is to the left, topped by a collection of buildings) the walker must detour from the Red Trail, getting above the treeline.

of Partenkirchen, the more picturesque of the two. The town is famous for its New Year's Day ski jumping event (one of the Four Hills' competition) and as a winter sports centre. It hosted the ski world championships in 1978, and will do so again in 2011.

The Purple Trail continues west into the Ammer Alps, and then heads north to Linderhof, where Ludwig II of Bavaria constructed a sumptuous palace (or rather enlarged an existing building) in the style of Versailles. Ludwig is today perhaps best known as the patron of Richard Wagner and his palace is one of the foremost tourist attractions in Bavaria. In the next section of the walk, after further alpine walking, you pass the castles of Neuschwanstein and Hohenschwangau before the trail drops down into Schwangau and Füssen.

The fairy-tale appearance of Schloss Neuschwanstein (the New Swan Stone Castle), also built by Ludwig II, has led to its being used as the model for castles in several theme parks, including the original Disneyland in the USA. Hohenschwangau Castle was built by Ludwig's father, Maximilian II; it was Ludwig's childhood home and his main home after his father's death. In the early 1950s the two castles were partially responsible for travel agents defining the road from Füssen to Würzburg as the Romantische Straße (Romantic Road), as it passed much that was deemed to portray German culture. The road itself is much older, having been the Roman Via Claudia Augusta. Schwangau is a cute little village, often overlooked by travellers heading for Füssen. At 2,650ft (808m), Füssen is Bavaria's highest town, and has much to admire. The church of St Magnus has a tenth–

ABOVE Aerial view of the Tiroler Lech Nature Park, a marvellous area of wooded hills crossed by the Red Trail.
BELOW The Purple Trail crossing the flank of the Fuchkarspitze to reach the Red Trail at Prinz-Luitpold Haus.

OPPOSITE Prinz-Luitpold Haus (at the bottom of the photograph) nestles below Hochvogel. The combined Red and Purple trails round the jagged crags that rise above the hut and follow the valley which heads out of the shot.

century fresco and a relic bone of Magnus, the town's patron saint, who is celebrated annually during a week-long festival which includes the sale of Magnus wine, production of which is limited to just 500 bottles.

From Füssen the Purple Trail climbs to the Austrian–German border, and you follow this, with the aid of a chain on one difficult section, to Falkenstein (4,156ft/1,267m), Germany's oldest castle. Built in the thirteenth century, the castle was ruinous by the nineteenth century. It was bought by Ludwig II, who intended to build another fairy-tale castle on the ruins but died before work could start. There are terrific views from the castle before the descent to Pfronten.

The trail now enters its final section, climbing through woodland to craggy Aggenstein (6,517ft/1,987m) on the national border, and detouring briefly through Austria before reaching the magnificent Allgäu Alps close to the Gaishorn (7,370ft/2,247m). From there an occasionally devious path follows the ridge line (which doubles as the national border) before descending west to the Prinz-Luitpold Haus (refuge), where it joins the Red Trail. You now follow the Red Trail (more or less: see below) to Oberstdorf.

THE RED TRAIL

The Bavarian section of the Red Trail is much shorter, but makes its way through sensational country, more than making up in quality for what it lacks in length. It enters Germany at the Meiler refuge (7,790ft/2,375m), which you reach after a climb, up steep scree, of over 3,900ft (1,200m) through fabulous rock scenery, at the end of a long day that began at Scharnitz, an Austrian Tyrol village above which looms the rock architecture of the Karwendel. The walk from the refuge is a welcome relief after that long first day (which can be split by staying overnight in the Leutasch valley), descending initially to the Schachen refuge, beyond which there are views over the Reintal and Zugspitze. The descent now continues more steeply, in part on an engineered path, and then through woods to the Bock refuge (3,451ft/1,052m); then it climbs gently through the Reintal with towering peaks on both sides to reach the Reintalanger refuge (4,480ft/1,366m).

From the refuge the walk crosses the Partnach stream, which flows down the Reintal, and then the source of the stream itself as it climbs to the Knorr refuge (6,727ft/2,051m). Ahead now is Zugspitze, at 9,715ft (2,962m) the highest peak in Germany. You can climb it as a detour – either all the way or using the cable car from Zugspitzplatt – but the Red Trail turns south along a contouring path to reach the national border at Gatterl (6,639ft/2,024m). Looking towards Zugspitze from here the eye is drawn to the high, arid plateau, a rock desert, of Zugspitzplatt. After a short climb to Feldernjöchl

Prinz-Luitpold Haus.

Beyond Prinz-Luitpold Haus there is a choice of routes on the combined Via Alpina trails, either by going downhill through the Oytal, or staying high on the valley's northern side to reach Edmund-Probst Haus and the cable car to Oberstdorf. This photograph was taken on the latter alternative, looking back along the valley side.

(6,708ft/2,045m) there is a descent to Seebenalm, where there is a view east to the Karwendel and the high peaks around the Grossglockner, and south to the Stubai and Ötztal Alps. The descent passes a Pestkapelle (Plague Chapel), one of many raised in the nineteenth century when plague ravaged Austria; with country people reluctant to visit churches in local towns and villages, as had been the custom, the chapels allowed a few families to gather and worship in relative safety. From the chapel the trail climbs steeply to the Coburger refuge.

The next two stages of the trail are westwards through Austria, beginning with a descent into Biberweir; this requires care, particularly the final section, which is both steep and can be treacherous. Then there is a steady climb through woodland to Grubig Alm and the Wolfratshauser refuge (5,740ft/1,750m). The second stage starts with a short climb, and then undulates gently to the Rotlech reservoir, hidden in trees and with views to rocky peaks. You continue downhill to Weissenbach in the Lech valley. The town is delightfully positioned, spreading along the river and ringed by high peaks. In medieval times Weissenbach was a storage depot on the salt route to western Austria,

its importance giving it the right to hold a market, so that it became a significant local centre. Today it is renowned for its annual carnival as well as being at the heart of the Tiroler Lech Nature Park, which covers the river from Steeg to Vils and also includes some side valleys. The park was set up to protect the river valley and its wildlife from overdevelopment, and includes cycleways and footpaths to allow visitors to explore a beautiful stretch of river.

The trail follows the Lech from the town, and then bears west away from it, staying in the Lech Park as it heads towards the Allgäu Alps. The view is dominated by the Hochvogel (8,505ft/2,593m). Soon the gentle valley walking is replaced by steeper terrain on the climb to Bockkarscharte, north of Hochvogel. Here you re-enter Germany, descending steeply to reach the Prinz-Luitpold Haus and the Purple Trail.

Both trails now follow a good path westwards to a junction below Himmeleck (7,055ft/2,151m), where they part company. The Red Trail turns left to follow an eroded path that descends straightforwardly into Oberstdorf, a rather unsatisfactory end to the Bavarian section of the route. Far better is to follow the Purple Trail, which turns right along a fine mountain path, and then using a cable for aid you cross a rock face below the Lachenkopf (6,931ft/2,113m) to reach the Edmund-Probst Haus (refuge). From here you can choose to avoid the final descent into Oberstdorf by using the cable car.

Close to the Edmund-Probst Haus there is a marvellous view over the Seealpsee into the Oytal valley, and to the Allgäu Alps beyond.

Travel

By air Flights are available to Salzburg and Innsbruck in Austria, and to Munich in Germany.

By rail Salzburg and Munich are linked to all major European cities by rail. From Salzburg a line runs to Berchtesgaden. You can also reach Berchtesgaden, Garmisch-Partenkirchen and Oberstdorf by rail from Munich.

By road Motorways link Munich with Salzburg and Innsbruck, and there are good roads deep into many of the valleys of the Bavarian Alps.

Maps and guides

There is, at present, no guide to either the Red or Purple Via Alpina Trails, though it is anticipated that these will become available over the next few years. The Via Alpina website (via-alpina.org) has a series of pdfs that may be downloaded, giving details of the suggested daily stages. The pdfs include the route profile and map (rudimentary, but adequate for tracing on the relevant Kompass 1:50,000 map), together with section times and the Kompass map number. There is also a brief description of the stage, but this is too brief to be of any real value, so you are left to explore, which adds to the sense of adventure (though may not be to everyone's taste).

The following Kompass Wander-, Bike- und Skitourenkarte 1:50,000 maps are essential and cover the entire trails (larger-scale maps are, of course, also available):

Purple Trail: Travelling from east to west (as in the text above), nos. 14, 10, 8, 6 and 4.
Red Trail: Again travelling from east to west, nos. 5, 4 and 3.

Waymarking

The routes are marked frequently with the standard red and white stripes. There are also frequent Via Alpina signs, with the appropriate colour tag, fixed to standard signposts. In general signage is excellent.

Accommodation

The idea of the Via Alpina is stage walking between mountain refuges. However, some stages are long and involve considerable climbing, and may tax the average walker. That said, if you prepare properly, using the website pdfs and the relevant maps, you can avoid camping. Those

who prefer camping should note that wild camping is banned in Germany. There are a number of excellent campsites in Bavaria, always accessible by road and so therefore usually in valleys, which can be used to split long stages.

Equipment

Each of the Bavarian trails is a high mountain route requiring good equipment, particularly excellent wet weather equipment. The mountains can also be cold, so be prepared for chilly weather even in the summer. There are no glacier crossings, so ice axe and crampons are not necessary, but, as always, hard, snowy winters can leave snow in hollows and gullies well into the summer, so caution is required. If in doubt, turn back – there is always tomorrow.

Climate

Bavaria has a central European climate. This means cold winters and hot summers, but, as usual, mountains influence the climate. In general, in summer the Allgäu Alps are wetter than those to the east.

Hazards

None, other than those usually associated with high mountain terrain. However, there are sections of eroded path that can be very slippery during or after wet weather and these require care. There are also sections that use *in situ* cables to aid progress across difficult, exposed terrain. These can present problems for walkers without sure feet and a head for heights.

TOP The lower Oytal is an excellent place for flowers and butterflies.
ABOVE Bavarian gentian.
RIGHT Bee pollinating restharrow.

LEFT Each evening in summer cows are brought from the alpine meadows through
Oberstdorf to their night quarters.

National Parks and Wildlife

Walkers on the Via Alpina will soon become familiar with the change in tree species with altitude, the dwarf mountain pine taking over from other conifers above about 6,000ft (about 1,800m). The alpine meadows will be awash with flowers – gentians, orchids – in spring, while you may see edelweiss in remote areas. It is more often seen in the Allgäu Alps. Please remember that picking edelweiss is forbidden.

The Berchtesgaden National Park, the only German Alpine National Park, was established in 1978 and covers 82 sq. miles (210 sq. km) of forest mountains and deep gorges, as well as less rugged country. Over fifty species of mammal have been identified in the park; those you are most likely to see include marmot, chamois, red deer and alpine ibex (steinbock). The latter are unlikely to have been natives of the area: the present stock was introduced in the 1930s for hunting. They were never very numerous and the park now holds only sixty to eighty animals. More rarely seen park mammals include both pine and beech martens. Over a hundred nesting bird species have been recorded. Most visitors hope to catch sight of the elusive golden eagle, but other unusual species include the northern goshawk, hazel and black grouse, and capercaillie, as well as a good collection of ducks and waders.

Chamois and marmot can be seen on other sections of the trails: chamois are often seen in the Allgäu Alps. Ibex are frequently seen near the Benediktenwand, as mentioned above. On damp mornings, you may also spot either of the common European salamanders. Fire salamanders, which are widespread across Europe, are usually seen at lower altitudes, while alpine salamanders, found throughout the Alps, prefer higher ground.

ABOVE Fire salamander.

OPPOSITE
LEFT ABOVE Alpine ibex.
LEFT BELOW Moss campion with painted lady, peacock and red admiral butterflies.
RIGHT ABOVE Dark green fritillary.
RIGHT CENTRE Marbled ringlet. On the last day into Oberstdorf there were swarms of these in the lower Oytal.
RIGHT BELOW Cardinal.

Partnachklamm

WETTERSTEIN ALPS, GERMANY

Across the Alps there are many examples of tight gorges carved by streams or rivers awash with meltwater, and in some cases the careful construction of walkways has opened these to visitors. Of these gorge walks, none is better than that of the Partnach River. The Partnach rises at the head of the Reintal, the wide valley enclosed by the huge walls of the Zugspitze/Höllentalspitze and peaks of the Teufelsgrat. Once it carried the outflowing stream of the Schneeferner, the now long-gone glacier that filled the valley during and immediately after the last Ice Age. Today the river flows partially underground before exiting the Reintal at the Bock Hut. It then flows north, passing through two smaller gorges and joining the Ferchenbach River, which drains the Ferchensee, a mountain lake west of Mittenwald. The combined rivers then flow through the Partnachklamm. After exiting this gorge, the river flows through the village of Partenkirchen, the village at the 'water gateway' (from which the name 'Partnach' derives). Partenkirchen is the more picturesque of the two settlements now combined (in name at least) into Garmisch-Partenkirchen.

In ancient times the Partnach was used as a supply route for timber felled on the mountain. After felling, the trees were sawn into logs of about 4ft (1.2m). An owner's mark was then added to the trunk and the log was thrown into the river to be floated down to the village for use as firewood, for charcoal making or for building. Spring was the best time for the work, as the river was highest then, and usually powerful enough to ensure the logs reached Partenkirchen. But the short logs and water pressure were not enough to prevent the

OPPOSITE and BELOW Winter in the gorge.

133

LEFT and OPPOSITE Summer in the gorge.
BELOW The river which runs through the gorge is home to dippers. But to the astonishment of many walkers, the birds – which feed by 'walking' underwater – remain throughout the winter, braving the chilling water.

attracting many visitors, regularly cause damage to the gorge and tunnels, necessitating further work each spring. In 1991 a huge rock fall, which fortunately injured no one, necessitated the construction of a new tunnel section.

To visit the gorge, and enjoy a fine walk with mountain views, start at the car park close to the Olympic stadium in Garmisch. From here the Eckbauerbahn cable car can be used to eliminate the uphill section of the walk, which takes the signed road for Wamberg at the far end of the car park. The drivable road soon ends and a track continues to this very pleasant village, from where a path continues, steeply at times, to the hilltop. Continue past the top station of the cable car – or exit here if that is the way you arrived – to reach the Berggasthof (mountain guest house/restaurant) Eckbauer and a view of the peaks of the Wetterstein.

The route now follows a well-signed and part-engineered path downhill through woodland to reach pleasant open alpine meadow and, passing more chances for refreshment, finally, the river. Turn right to reach the klamm or gorge. Tunnels and safe walkways now take you through it, past spectacular views of the rushing river and the occasional curtain of water cascading down the cliffs. The gorge is about 750 yards (700m) long but only a few metres wide in places, the cliffs up to 265ft (80m) high. At the exit from the gorge a modest fee is payable.

It is now just a matter of following the road back to the Olympic stadium, but those tired of walking can take a horse and carriage for a rather less modest fee.

occasional log-jam. If that occurred, a man sitting in a special chair with a roof to deflect falling rocks would be lowered into the gorge and, using a long hook, attempt to disturb the jam and get the logs moving again. It was brutal, dangerous work, and in the last years of the nineteenth century a walkway was constructed: steel anchors attached to the rock face allowed wooden boards to be laid, from which men could reach the logs safely with long poles.

Soon afterwards, adventurous visitors began to use the walkway. Sensing the economic advantages of the gorge, the local alpine club began to blast the tunnels visitors now used. By the 1930s the walkway was completed, but annual ice formations, while spectacular and

Walk information

Map: Kompass 1:30,000 sheet 790, but non-scaled, though adequate. Maps including the route can also be obtained from the local Tourist Office.

Start/finish: the Olympic stadium, Garmisch-Partenkirchen. Length: 6 miles (10km) for the full route, 4 miles (6.5km) if the cable car is used. Ascent: 1,600ft (500m) if the full route is walked. The descent is also, of course, 1,600ft (500m).

The Stubai Horseshoe

AUSTRIA

A casual look at a relief map suggests Austria's mountains form a continuous chain, dominating the west of the country and continuing through the southern half. But differences in rock architecture do exist, and deep valleys also separate the chain into discrete mountain blocks. One such block, the Stubai Alps, can be found to the south-west of Innsbruck, a beautiful old city in western Austria. The Stubai are bounded to the east by the valley of the Sill River, through which snakes the A13 (E45) motorway descending from the Brenner Pass to Innsbruck, and to the west by the Ötztal, the valley that has given its name to the mountain mass to its west. The Inn valley defines a northern boundary, while to the south are peaks that form the border between Italy and Austria, a border defined after the First World War when Italy occupied an area granted to it under the Treaty of London in 1915, but also annexed a section of ethnically German Tyrol which lay south of the alpine watershed.

The Stubai Alps are the most compact of Austria's mountain areas. This, together with the fact that the peaks are liberally dotted with high-level huts which offer accommodation and meals, and the topography of the area, a horseshoe of peaks around an easily accessible valley, make it ideal for the walker. As one of the shortest mountain walks in this book, the horseshoe is also ideal for those setting out on their first long-distance path (but with the proviso of the aided sections noted below). However, despite the comfort and hospitality offered by the huts, the Stubaier Höhenweg, the Stubai High Route, is not a trivial exercise. Winter snows can lie long into the summer in certain areas, making the walking potentially hazardous, and as with all high mountain areas – the high Stubai peaks rise to around 11,500ft (3,500m) – the weather can be unpredictable, sudden squalls turning a pleasant day in the hills into a far less agreeable experience. There are also sections of scrambling and others where fixed wire ropes aid progress. These sections require a head for heights and sure-footedness, and have been known to scare walkers with limited climbing experience.

Two routes are possible. The one described here is the walker's route, a relatively straightforward eight- or nine-day trek. The second route, which involves glacier crossing, is a more exacting outing requiring alpine experience and climbing equipment and the ability to use it. Only brief details of this second option are given here.

For the walker interested in geology, the routes are interesting. The high Stubai, the southern and south-western area traversed by the routes, comprise igneous rocks, gneisses and granites, while the start and end of the routes, the western and northern section, are limestone. This mix of rock offers a contrast between high, glaciated mountains and lower but sharp and angular peaks, so that the area is continuously picturesque.

The Stubaier Höhenweg starts in the Stubaital, a valley due south of Innsbruck, but it is worth making a tour of the old city before beginning the walk. The city's old centre is an architectural gem, the Goldenes Dachl (Golden Roof) being the highlight. Originally constructed in the fifteenth century as the seat of Tyrolean rulers, the roof of the name was added in about 1500 by the Holy Roman Emperor Maximilian I. Beneath the 2,657 copper tiles the Emperor would watch tournaments in the square below. If time permits, seek out the Hofkirche, built in Gothic style by Ferdinand I as a memorial to Maximilian, his grandfather, and housing his cenotaph, which is renowned for its sculpture. The city has twice hosted the Winter Olympics, and will host the inaugural Winter Youth Olympics in 2012; and it is home to one leg of the annual Four Hills ski jumping competition, the new jump built in 2003 on Bergisel, a hill to the south of the city, being a local landmark. Innsbruck is also home to the Austrian Alpine Club, which has an interesting Alpine Museum.

The Stubaier Höhenweg starts at Neder, a village in Stubaital, reached by bus from Innsbruck. The walk begins along a single track road (signed as Path 123) up the Pinnistal, a side valley which heads into the limestone peaks of the Kirchdach, the prominent peaks being Kirchdachspitze (9,315ft/2,840m) and Habicht (10,749ft/3,277m). The walls of the Kirchdachspitze are a magnet for rock climbers, though the rock is rather more brittle than many might wish. You can avoid the walk up the track by using a minibus which transports walkers to Pinnisalm; this cuts the distance to the Innsbrucker Hut in half and reduces a climb of 4,600ft (1,400m) to 2,600ft (800m). Beyond Pinnisalm, which is often crowded, the crowd thins significantly. The view ahead is dominated by Habicht as the climb starts, gradually at first and then more steeply up a zigzagging path to the hut. The Innsbrucker is owned by the Österreichischer Alpenverein (the Austrian Alpine Club, known as the ÖAV) and can accommodate over a hundred walkers/climbers; many of the latter use it as a base for an ascent of Habicht (which requires a glacier crossing). The hut's restaurant is excellent.

From the Innsbrucker, which is set on the Pinnisjoch at 7,770ft (2,369m), the next hut is the Bremer, to which it is officially a six-hour walk that includes a couple of relatively demanding aided sections. Do not be deceived by the official time: this is a long day, and an early start and enough food and drink to keep body and soul together are recommended. From the hut the Stubaier Höhenweg follows Path 124, climbing to a col at 8,394ft (2,559m) and then maintaining altitude, with one aided section, before a steep aided descent. Now it climbs (often across snow, even in late summer) to a col at 8,495ft

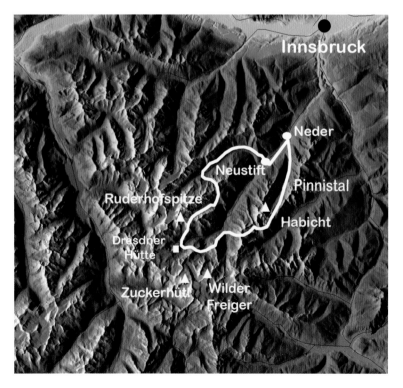

(2,590m) from where the next objective, the Bremer Hut, is visible. An aided descent reaches the Lauterersee before a final aided section to the hut. The Bremer Hut (7,915ft/2,413m) is owned by the Deutscher Allpenverein (DAV) and is delightfully situated beside a small lake with a backdrop of high Stubai peaks.

From the Bremer a much shorter day's walking takes you to the Nürnberger Hut. Following Path 102 south-west, you soon climb steeply (aided) to the Simmingjochl (9,033ft/2,754m), from where there is a fine view of the Austrian–Italian border ridge to the south. The hut at the col is used by border police. An aided descent reaches a (usually snow-filled) gully, beyond which the Nürnberger Hut is visible. An aided descent and a plank bridge crossing of the Langtal River lead to a final scramble to the hut (7,478ft/2,280m). As the name indicates, the hut is owned by the Nürnberg section of the DAV and was built in the late nineteenth century in fine style, with some amazing features including a fountain in the excellent dining room. The hut can accommodate around 150 people, and is often crowded, as it is the start point of climbs on the high border ridge peaks, and of the most popular of the Stubai glacier routes (see below).

The walk continues along Path 102, climbing gradually and then very steeply up aided rock slabs to the Niederl pass (8,617ft/2,627m). A steep aided descent leads to a small lake; then the path continues

ABOVE An aerial view of Habicht. The route goes up Pinnistal, the valley left of the peak, to reach the Innsbrucker Hut, just out of sight on Pinnisjoch.
BELOW The Nürnberger Hut.

ABOVE The Sulzenau Hut sits close to the Blaue Lacke, to the left of the photograph. The Dresdner Hut is at the top of the cable car to the right of the photograph. Peiljoch, which must be crossed to link the two huts is a pass on the ridge in the centre.

RIGHT At the Peiljoch there is a whole city of stone cairns.

A view to the Fernerstube and Sulzenauferner glaciers with, ahead, Rundsheim and, right, Wilder Freiger and Wilder Pfaff, from Peiljoch. The Sulzenau Hut is down the valley to the left.

across much easier ground, with fine views of the Wilder Freiger, to the Sulzenau Hut (7,186ft/2,191m), another large DAV hut. Built in the 1970s to replace an original destroyed in an avalanche, the hut is popular with climbers heading for the Zuckerhütl, Stubai's highest peak, and with climbing schools of both ÖAV and DAV.

The next section from the Sulzenau to the Dresdner Hut is also quite short, though a little more exacting. The route follows Path 102 south-west from the hut, ignoring Path 136, which heads off left after a short distance. It continues past rock faces popular with climbing schools, and then follows the right-hand (true left) moraine edge of the Sulzenau Glacier. The moraine heaps are an indication of the glacier's shrinkage, the ice now being well over a half-mile (actually about 1km) further back towards Zuckerhütl. There are aided sections here, but the going is reasonably straightforward: you ignore the signed path for Zuckerhütl and bear right (north-west) up a steep path to the Peiljoch (8,777ft/2,676m), from where there is a magnificent view of high peaks and the Sulzenauferner (Sulzenau Glacier), as well as a closer view of an extraordinary collection of stone cairns – an entire city of them. The descent from Peiljoch starts comfortably, but steepens, and includes an aided section. At a path junction a route comes in from the right: this is an alternative path from the Sulzenau which is worth considering if time permits, as it has the advantage of reaching the summit of the Grosser Trögler (9,515ft/2,901m), named for a local guide who was killed in a climbing accident – a slightly higher viewpoint of the Zuckerhütl.

The way ahead is now obvious, the top station of the cable car from the head of the Stubaital and the Dresdner Hut being visible, and continues more straightforwardly downhill to the hut (7,552ft/2,302m). The hut was originally built in the 1870s by the

Dresden section of the DAV, but has been enlarged several times. Its once idyllic surroundings have now been somewhat compromised by the machinery of the skiing industry. The hut is closed in winter, but summer walkers will be joined by day trippers using the cable car to access higher ground. It is difficult to complain about people wanting to share the hut and its environment, but walkers will almost certainly enjoy the peace that descends as the last cable car heads down to the valley.

The next day's walk is a long one: you need to set out early and allow at least seven hours. The route starts by following Paths 102/138 west, and then bears right (north) along Path 138. It now descends into the Wilder Grube (the 'wild gully'), at first steeply down an aided section and then more gradually. The gully collects water from numerous streams and these have to be negotiated to reach a path that climbs through beautiful alpine meadow to reach a small lake at Hohe Grube. The view north towards the border peaks is excellent from here, as is the view ahead as the path skirts the southern side of the Ruderhofspitze.

The route now reaches its wildest section, a series of high cols, the negotiating of which is usually aided. Rotten snow and loose rock can make both navigation and walking difficult, so you need to take care. The first col (at about 9,000ft/2,750m) on a ridge south of the Gamsspitze is straightforward. The second, between the Gamsspitze and the Schafspitze, at about the same altitude, has an aided descent over steep rocks. The third, the Grawagrubennieder (9,450ft/2,881m), is the highest on the Stubaier Höhenweg and requires care. The ascent is not a great problem and is marked with poles, but the descent is over loose rock. Rockslips also obscure the correct route to the snout of the Hochmoosferner (Hochmoos Glacier). Shrinkage means that the

The peaks above the Neue Regensberger Hut. From left to right: Ruderhofspitze, Seespitze, Kraulspitze and Knotenspitze.

glacier crossing is now short, but you need to be careful to follow the cairned route. Beyond the glacier the route is easier to follow, first to the lake of Falbesoner See and then along a path to the Neue Regensberger, another DAV hut, at 7,498ft/2,286m.

Following the arduous day spent reaching the Neue Regensberger Hut, it is a relief to discover that the next day is, perhaps, the easiest on the route, though not actually the shortest. The route follows Path 133 (the Dr Franz Höertnagl Weg, named, apparently, for the Director of Innsbruck General Hospital) through fine country, though with more limited views than you have become used to, to reach the Franz Senn Hut, owned by the ÖAV and named for a nineteenth-century Stubaital pastor who encouraged tourism to the area as a way of combating the chronic poverty of his parishioners, and was a founder member of both the ÖAV and DAV.

The final stage of the route is another long one – in distance terms the longest on the horseshoe – following Path 132 to its junction with Path 102/117, and then bearing right along the latter (the Franz Senn Weg) across undulating, occasionally rugged ground south of Schaldersspitze/Wildkopf, with great views back the way you have come. Welcome refreshments are available at the old chamois hunter's hut on Seducker Hochalm, neatly situated about halfway through the stage; then the route continues to the Sendersjöchl (8,125ft/2,477m), from where there is a fine, and almost final, view of the high Stubai.

Now the route climbs to Steinkogel (8,493ft/2,589m), descending a little to the Seejöchl (8,259ft/2,518m) and the final, slightly exposed walk to the DAV's Starkenburger Hut. From here, you descend to Neustift and buses back to Innsbruck.

The Franz Senn Hut.

THE GLACIER ROUTE

You can climb the high peaks of the Stubai by spending extra days at the huts of the Stubaier Höhenweg, using the huts as bases for out-and-back expeditions. Ice climbing equipment will be required, which increases both the time needed to complete the horseshoe walk and the weight that you have to carry along it.

An alternative is to make a shorter, glacier route from the Nürnberger Hut, ascending the Wilder Freiger (11,129ft/3,393m) and descending into Italy to overnight at Rifugio Regina Elena, a hut of the Verona section of the Italian Alpine Club (CAI). The hut (at 10,480ft/3,195m) was built in the late nineteenth century, but lost to Italy with the transfer of the South Tyrol after the First World War. It is commonly known as the Becherhaus on the Austrian side of the border. Now cross the upper section of the Übeltal Glacier to the Müller Hut from where you can climb the Wilder Pfaff (11,339ft/3,457m), with an out-and-back climb from the Pfaffensattel (10,968ft/3,344m) to the Zuckerhütl (at 11,503ft/3,507m the highest peak in the Stubai: it was first climbed in 1863 by Joseph Anton Specht and Alois Tanzer). Return to the saddle, cross the Pfaffen Glacier and descend to the Hildesheimer Hut. You can complete the short high-peak tour by following Path 102, an aided path, and crossing the Gaisskar Glacier to reach the Kiosk Jochdohle, from where you can climb the Schaufelspitze (10,929ft/3,332m). You can now descend to the Dresdner Hut, perhaps making use of the summer ski lifts.

ABOVE Zuckerhütl, right, and Wilder Pfaff. In recent years there has been much less *zucker* on the Zuckerhütl.

RIGHT The improbably sited Becherhaus on the Glacier Route.

Wildlife

The Stubai do not form part of a National Park, and the extensive year-round activity on such a compact range means that wildlife has inevitably taken second place. Marmots are the most likely mammals to be seen, particularly west of the Dresdner Hut above the Wilder Grube. Bird life tends to be sparse, but alpine choughs may be seen. The plant lover will find the Stubai much more appealing: an array of alpine species may be found here, including Clusius's gentian, alpine and common pasque flowers, mountain avens, ox-eye daisy, arnica, alpine aster, the magnificent martagon lily and, of course, edelweiss.

RIGHT Edelweiss.
BELOW Martagon lily.

OPPOSITE
LEFT ABOVE Alpine chough.
LEFT BELOW Burnt orchid.
RIGHT ABOVE Greater butterfly orchid.
RIGHT BELOW Spring gentian.

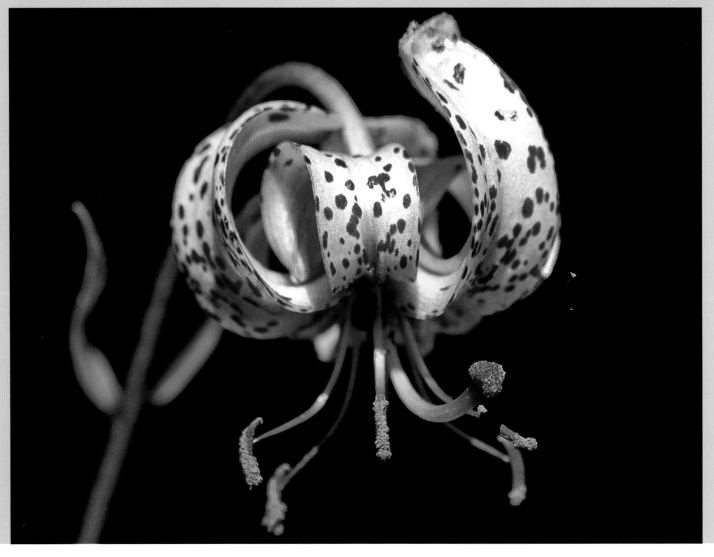

Travel

By air There are regular budget airline flights to Innsbruck, the closest airport. There is a bigger selection of flights from the UK to Munich, from where Innsbruck can be reached by road or rail.

By rail Innsbruck is on main rail links across Europe, with connections to Munich and Paris.

By road Innsbruck has a motorway connection to Munich, from where there is connection to the German autobahn system and the motorway systems of France and Belgium. Buses link Innsbruck with the starting village of Neder, and with the finishing village of Neustift.

Maps and guides

Trekking in the Stubai Alps, Allan Hartley, Cicerone.

There is no single, named glacier route, but this excellent guide also includes a description of arguably the best of these, a longer route than that given here. The guide and the maps below are essential.

Kompass 1:50,000 Wander-, Bike- und Skitourenkarte sheet 83 (Stubaier Alpen).

The Austrian Alpine Club also publishes two 1:25,000 sheets covering the area: sheet 31/1 Stubai Alpen: Hoch Stubai and sheet 31/2 Stubai Alpen: Sellrain.

Waymarking

The walking routes of the Stubai are numbered, and these numbers are given on the maps and in the recommended guide. Signs for these route numbers are distributed along the route and are well maintained. Be sure to look for the route number you are on rather than expecting

ABOVE Signpost near the Dresdner Hut.
RIGHT Alpeinertal. the valley followed towards the end of the Horseshoe walk. In the lower centre of the photograph the Franz Senn Hut can be seen.

The Starkenberger Hut.

signs for the Stubaier Höhenweg, as it is not always mentioned on the signs. However, in the wilder areas of the route the paths can be indistinct. Red paint splashes on rocks help, but remnant snow can cover these. Guidebook and map are then essential.

Accommodation

The huts along both routes are owned and maintained by either the German or Austrian Alpine Clubs. To guarantee accommodation you will need to join the UK section of the Österrechischer Alpenverein. In theory you are allowed a stay of no more than three nights in a hut, but this rule is often relaxed if there is space available. Meals are served, and there are toilet and washing facilities (the latter now often with cold water only to minimize fuel usage), as well as a drying room for wet clothing. The huts named above are usually open from the end of June, or from July, until September.

Camping is allowed but, given the number and quality of the huts, is hardly worthwhile.

Equipment

A cotton or silk sleeping bag liner is essential, as the huts are phasing out the sheets that were once offered. Blankets are still available, though some walkers take their own lightweight sleeping bags in case they are in short supply. The Stubaier Höhenweg requires the usual walking equipment, windproof, wet-weather gear being essential, as this is a high mountain route and summer storms can bring low temperatures and chilling winds. On the glacier route, ice axes, crampons and a rope are essential, as is a limited amount of protection equipment.

Climate

As with all mountain areas, the weather you experience may well change from day to day. In summer, idyllic days are common, but so are sharp storms. Snow lies late on the Stubai, the Stubaier Höhenweg rarely being entirely free until late August/September. However, such snow as you encounter is unlikely to be a hazard except early in the season (June and, perhaps, early July).

Hazards

The well-positioned huts mean that bodily needs can be well catered for, so that the only real hazard is fatigue. Be careful not to overextend yourself; note the suggested times on the signposts and check your progress against them. The signs indicate walking time only, with no allowance for stops for any purpose. Personal experience suggests that the times are for a very fit walker – do not be discouraged.

The route has a number of aided sections and these can be tricky if there is still snow lying. In some places, particularly on the limestone of the eastern route, freeze-thaw can lead to loose rock, and falling rocks can be a hazard. Rockslips can also change the geography of the route, though these are likely to be minor.

Summer skiing is possible on the Stubai glaciers. To prevent collisions between skiers and walkers/climbers a Ruhezone (calm zone) exists, making downhill skiing off limits at certain times. In some places the Ruhezone lasts all year. But through misunderstanding or blatant disregard, skiers do occasionally breach the zone and walkers should keep an eye open for them.

Königsee and the Jenner

BERCHTESGADEN ALPS, GERMANY AND AUSTRIA

The Berchtesgaden National Park, covering an area of mountain south of the town that names it, extends to the German–Austrian border, and includes the Königsee (which is crossed on a Via Alpina – see page 114); consequently it has a wide range of habitats, enhancing its ecological importance. Above the lake's north-eastern tip rises the Jenner. The summit plateau of this 6,147ft (1,874m) peak was once forested, but felling and grazing have produced an alpine meadow. Above Königsee an engineered platform offers a majestic view of both the lake and the peaks of the Watzmann massif. Refuges have also been built, provide opportunities for food, drink and even a night's stay. To many that whole package may sound like a good reason to stay well clear, but the Jenner has so much to offer in terms of views, and there is so much mountain away from the crowds, that it cannot be overlooked.

The walk starts from the car park at Königsee village. Here hundreds of cars can, and are, parked by visitors heading for the Königsee steamer or for the Jennerbahn cable car, which lifts them to the top station restaurant close to the summit and viewing platform. The summit can be reached by walking too, and to walk either up or down allows you to explore more of the National Park. Here we use the cable car to ascend and take a leisurely stroll down the mountain to return.

OPPOSITE K nigsee and the Watzmann from the viewing platform below Jenner's summit.

BELOW Berchtesgaden and the Untersberg from Jenner's summit.

LEFT Königsee and the Berchtesgaden Alps from the summit of the Jenner. Having used the ferry to traverse the Königsee, the Via Alpina Purple Trail (see page 116) heads east, following the northern edge of the alps.

BELOW Carl von Stahl-Haus. The Jenner is extremely popular with Austrians, particularly those living in and around Salzburg. The border between Germany and Austria lies just a few metres from the refuge. allowing Austrians an impressive view of Salzburgerland (OPPOSITE).

From the top cable car station a path leads to the viewing platform – just follow the crowds! The path is not trivial, however, seemingly engineered to have the correct angle and correct covering of shaped gravel for walkers to feel they are traversing a steel plate covered with ball bearings. On each of my visits at least one visitor has slipped and fallen. The reward for the risk imposed by the path is a view that is breathtaking. The short scramble to the mountain's summit, adorned with a large cross, offers equally fine views of Berchtesgaden and the high peaks beyond it, and of the high tops of Hoher Göll to the northeast.

To descend, you follow the treacherous path, past the cable car's top station and continue west on a path that descends sharply to reach flatter ground. To the right is the Schneibsteinhaus, which has accommodation as well as serving refreshments, but it is best to bear left along a narrow path through tall vegetation to reach Carl von Stahl-Haus, another hut which is beautifully set on the border between Germany and Austria. A short walk leads to an excellent viewpoint into Salzburgerland.

There is now a choice. You can retrace your steps to the top station and use the cable car for the entire descent. Or you can retrace your steps to a sign that points the way to Mittelstation, descending past Mitterkasser Alm, where there are plenty of marmots (though as usual you are more likely to hear than see them). You can use the cable car

from the middle station, or continue the walk, heading north along Path 497 through woodland and bearing left at a path junction to reach a road. Then you turn left, but soon go left again on a path (the Stufenweg and Brandkopfweg) that rounds the southern slope of Brandkopf (3,792ft/1,156m) and descends steeply to the hamlet of Holz. Look out for paintings nailed to the trees as you descend: these are votive offerings, placed here to commemorate a fatality, usually in the hills, by grieving relatives. Look out, too, for the flowers for which the National Park is famous – alpenrose, the purple-red brown gentian and spotted gentian, from the roots of which gentian brandy was (and occasionally still is) distilled. On rocky ground it is also possible to spot edelweiss. In Holz, bear left along Richard-Voss-Strasse to return to the start.

Walk information

Map: Kompass (1:50,000 series) sheet 14. A map at about 1:20,000 is available from the Berchtesgaden Tourist Office – ask for the Berchtesgadener Land Ortsplan.
Start/finish: Königsee village. Length: full walk 4 miles (6.5km).
Ascent: 300ft (90m), but a descent of 2,100ft (650m) to Mittelstation. The full descent adds another 1,800ft (550m) and 2½ miles (4km) to the itinerary.

Alta Via 2

ITALY

During the last decade of the nineteenth century a French geologist who gloried in the name Déodat-Guy-Sylvain-Tancré de Gratet de Dolomieu was travelling in the Tyrol when he discovered a strange form of limestone. Unlike the limestones he normally encountered, Dolomieu found that when dropped into weak acid this form did not effervesce. After he had published his finding, the Swiss geologist Nicolas-Théodore de Saussure (son of Horace-Bénédict de Saussure of Mont Blanc fame) suggested that the new rock type should be named dolomie after its discoverer. In English the name was changed to dolomite.

Dolomite is a magnesium-rich limestone, found across the world but most famous for being the basis of the fabulous rock towers of northern Italy, specifically the area between the valleys of the Adige and Tagliamento rivers, and the offset Brenta Dolomites west of the Adige. Though the towers themselves are, in general, the playground of rock climbers, the passes between them, and the high plateaux from which, occasionally, they spring, provide some of the best walking and most spectacular viewpoints in the European uplands. No surprise then that the Dolomites have attracted long-distance walkers, and two marvellous routes have been threaded through the eastern Dolomites. Known by their Italian name, these two Alta Vie (high roads) are justifiably popular. AV1 – Alta Via 1 (vie is the plural of via) – links Lago di Braies to Belluno, passing the Cinque Torri, Monte Pelmo and Monte Civetta along the way. AV2 links Bressanone with Feltre, a journey of 115 miles (185km) involving 30,000ft (9,000m) of climbing, crossing the Sella and the Pale di San Martino, and passing the Marmolada. Each route has its supporters, but for me, the Sella and Pale plateaux, and the views from them, epitomize the Dolomites, and it is AV2 that I explore here.

Although officially AV2 starts from Valcroce, it is likely that you will visit, or spend the night in, the town of Bressanone, a short distance to the west (which is why I have given it as the start point above).

The town is certainly worth visiting. Settled at least 3,000 years ago, and later a Roman settlement, the town formally enters history in a document dating from 901, when it had the German name Brixen, a name still heard and given as an alternative on maps and in official writings. As Brixen, it was an important city of the Austrian Tyrol, becoming Italian and acquiring its new name in the post First World War settlement. Before leaving, you should visit Piazza Duomo and the surrounding streets to see the best of the exquisite old town.

From Bressanone you can take a bus to San Andrea and then the cable car to Valcroce, where AV2 begins with a climb to Rifugio Plose, set close to the summit of Monte Telegrafo (8,154ft/2,486m). The view from the rifugio is superb, and fine views are maintained on the descent to Passo Rodella (not to be confused with the more famous pass of the same name further south). From the pass, AV2 enters the Puez-Odle Nature Park. It then climbs high and stays high, outflanking the wall of the Walsicher Ring to reach the Forcella de Putia (7,731ft/2,357m) between it and Sass Putia. The walk now traverses the park, where the scenery is a mix of formidable rock towers and lush alpine pasture. You pass two rifugi (Genova and Puez), between which you spend a long day crossing a series of high passes, the dramatic Forcella della Roa, below spiky Piz Duleda (to the east/left), being the highest at 8,584ft (2,617m). The route now crosses an undulating rock plateau below the cliffs of the Piz de Puez, bearing

south around one spur of cliff that elbows its way on to the platform, to reach Rifugio Puez (8,118ft/2,475m), beautifully positioned in a true mountain wilderness. The refuge is remote, so much so that it can only be supplied by helicopter.

Beyond the refuge AV2 crosses Forcella de Ciampei (7,760ft/2,366m) to reach the Altipano de Crespeina and the green lake that shares its name. One of the highlights of the route is now ahead: the vast (and vastly impressive) Gruppo del Sella, revealed from the Forcella de Crespeina (8,292ft/2,528m), and dominating the view as you follow a route that threads a devious path through a series of weathered spikes and pinnacles to reach Passo Gardena (6,957ft/2,121m).

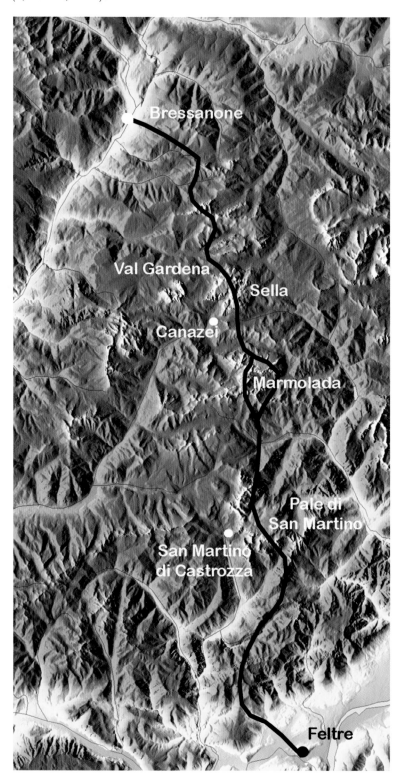

Street market in the old centre of Bressanone.

Ahead now is one of the finest day walks in the Dolomites. To the left of Berghaus Frara is a path that rises easily towards the huge wall of the Sella, before bearing east below it. At a signpost the route turns north into Val Setus, following a steep, zigzagging path up steep scree and then continuing up a cable-aided cliff to reach the Sella plateau and Rifugio Pisciadú. Now it follows the eastern shore of the lake below the hut, before climbing, occasionally aided, to another sign which points not towards the cleft in the peaks ahead, as might be expected, but to the right, up on to a ridge above the plateau. Then the route descends and round the rock humps ahead to reach Rifugio Boè. From there, a well-trodden path (Boè being the destination for most day-trippers on the Pordoi cable car) traverses below Piz Boè to reach Rifugio Forcella del Pordoi. From here many walkers climb to the top station of the Pordoi cable car for a swift descent to Passo Pordoi, avoiding a knee-jarring scree descent.

The pass is a tourist magnet, with the shops etc. that such a place implies. AV2 leaves at the Albergo Savoia, bearing right by the chapel and climbing to Rifugio Baita Fedarola and on to Rifugio Viél dal Pan (7,977ft/2,432m), named for the walk AV2 follows as it traverses from Pordoi to Lago di Fedáia. The name translates as 'bread walk' and dates from the nineteenth century when the Venetian Republic attempted to monopolize the grain trade from southern Italy and enterprising locals set up a grain-smuggling route through the mountains to avoid punitive taxes. The walk also offers the possibility of seeing – or more likely hearing – marmots, particularly close to Rifugio Fedarola.

Lago di Fedáia is curious in being not one but two lakes separated by moraine deposits. The eastern, much smaller, lake was formed behind deposits left by glacial retreat, the moraine also forming a natural barrier when in 1956 a huge dam wall, about half a mile (800m) long and 200ft (60m) high, was built to provide a water source for a hydro-electric power station generating 20MW. The original lake (or, more precisely, the pass at its eastern edge) was once the border between the Venetian Republic and the Austrian Brixen Principality, which explains the smuggling traffic on the Viél dal Pan.

At the lake the Marmolada blocks all progress southwards. At 10,968ft (3,343m) the peak is the highest in the Dolomites and has, on its northern flank, the only large glacier in the range. The highest point, Punta Penia, lies at the western end of a long, gently descending ridge which has four more prominences over 3,000m – Punta Rocca

ABOVE Looking down into Val Badia from the Sella plateau.
RIGHT At Passo Pordoi there is a memorial to Fausto Coppi (1919–60), the great Italian cyclist who won the Giro d'Italia five times, the Tour de France twice and was World Champion in 1953.

OPPOSITE
ABOVE A steep, loose path takes AV2 up Val Setus to reach the Sella plateau.
BELOW On the Sella plateau.

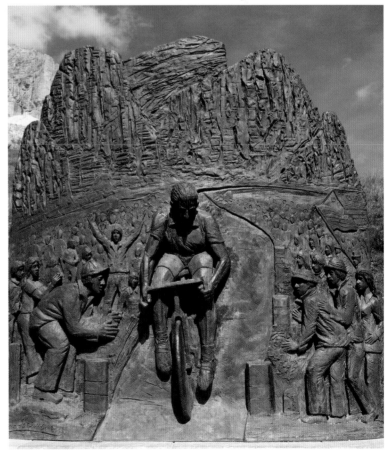

Looking south from Rifugio Forcella Pordoi. AV2 descends the steep gully to Passo Pordoi, then follows an old smuggling route across the ridge at the centre of the photograph to reach the Marmolada, the mountain bulk left of centre.

(10,854ft/3,309m), Punta Ombretta (10,594ft/3,230m), Monte Serauta (10,066ft/3,069m) and Punta Serauta (9,955ft/3,035m). Punta Penia was first climbed on 28 September 1864 by the Austrian Paul Grohmann and the Dimai brothers, two local guides. From the peak's eastern side a cable car rises to a top station close to Punta Rocca, with impressive views of the glacier, the Ghiacciaio della Marmolada.

AV2 avoids the peak by staying close to the main road over the Passo di Fedáia to Malga Ciapéla, and then skirting Monte Fop to reach the Forca Rossa (8,167ft/2,490m), beyond which it descends to Rifugio Fuchiade. Climbers may prefer a more direct route. For this, glacier equipment is required. To follow this variant, take the cable car from the western end of the lake, and follow path 606 downhill westwards, and then south-west to reach the edge of a small glacier. You will need steel-hard ice crampons and a rope to reach the Forcella de la Marmolada (9,545ft/2,910m). From here a *via ferrata* heads up the peak's western ridge to Punta Penia. Full ice climbing equipment is required here, as well as a *via ferrata* kit, as the upper reaches of the mountain can be ice-encrusted even if the weather is good. From the

pass, *via ferrata* kit is also essential, as the route makes a 65ft (20m) descent of an aided, vertical rock wall.

When, on 23 May 1915, Italy entered the First World War by declaring war on Austria, the border between the Hapsburg Empire and Italy followed what is now the border of Trentino with Lombardy and Veneto, a switchback line that links peaks and passes of the Dolomites. Along this tortuous border Austrian and Italian soldiers fought not only each other but the terrible weather of the high Dolomites. Winter cold killed many, while avalanches added another hazard. This conflict was nicknamed the Guerra Bianca (the White War) by those engaged in it. Beneath the Marmolada's glacier Austrian miners excavated around 5 miles (8km) of tunnels and rooms in the ice and, occasionally, the rock that underlay it, creating enough space to house a battalion, while along the high frontier trenches were carved in the ice or, on lower ground, the earth. Cableways were constructed to lift ammunition and other supplies from the valleys; the technology developed was later adapted to the carrying of skiers and walkers. The White War also saw the development of ice pitons, which were to revolutionize ice climbing, while the metal ladders and wire ropes used to protect soldiers on sheer or exposed cliffs are now the basis of the *vie ferrata*.

The fighting was intense, often in the form of hand-to-hand combat as outflanking manoeuvres resulted in trenches changing sides. It is estimated that many thousands of men died. Today the glacier still occasionally yields bones and military hardware. Rifugio Contrin (6,612ft/2,016m), which lies at the base of the path that descends from the pass, has a collection of shell cases, helmets and other items found locally; the ladder too dates from the White War. The area around the *rifugio* has still-discernible shell holes, while the path AV2 follows from it passes the remains of barbed-wire fortifications and even a decaying artillery platform. This path leads to Passo delle Cirelle (8,800ft/2,683m), from where a descent reaches Rifugio Fuchiade and the alternative route.

From Fuchiade, AV2 follows easy tracks to Passo di San Pellegrino. It then rounds the porphyry mass of Col Margherita (8,144ft/2,483m), its igneous origin explaining its lumpy appearance, to reach Passo di Vallès, from where there is a fabulous view east to the Civetta and, to the north, Monte Pelmo. The Alta Via is now heading for the Pale di San Martino, the second of the high Dolomite plateaux. The view as

Memories of the 'White War'.

BELOW *Via ferrata* constructed during the war. The 'iron way' now helps walkers down a steep cliff to gain the Val Rosalia and Rifugio Contrin.
LEFT Gun emplacement on Cima Cadine near the Marmolada.
BELOW LEFT Shells and other items unearthed nearby on display in Rifugio Contrin.

Evening light on the Sassolungo from Rifugio Contrin.

you advance towards the Forcella di Venegia takes in the Cimon della Pala (10,444ft/3,184m), the Cima della Vezzana (10,470ft/3,192m) and the chain of summits, each a little lower than the one to its right, heading north-east towards Monte Mulaz (9,532ft/2,906m). Beyond another high pass (Passo di Venegiota, 7,554ft/2,303m) the route passes below the eastern face of Monte Mulaz to reach the impressively sited Rifugio Mulaz, with the rock towers of Cima del Focobon towering above it.

The route from the *rifugio* requires good weather and sure-footedness, for although it is well signed, it is exposed in places. There are aid cables, but the inexperienced, or those new to exposed positions, will find the walk nerve-racking, and very much more so if poor weather means you have to search out the route. If conditions are

poor, it is best to head west from the *rifugio*, crossing Passo del Mulaz and dropping down to the Passo Rolle. Indeed, you can avoid the whole walk section from Pass di Vallès by heading for Passo Rolle, from where you can use a bus to reach San Martino di Castrozza and a cable car that will lift you to the edge of the high plateau.

The route itself heads towards Passo del Mulaz, but then bears left and steeply up a scree path to reach Forcella Margherita (8,708ft/2,655m). You now have to cross the amphitheatre below to reach the Passo delle Farangole (9,617ft/2,932m), the highest point of Alta Via 2, a narrow pass between the enormous rock towers of Cima del Focobon (10,017ft/3,054m) and Cima di Val Grande (9,965ft/3,038m). Those viewing the pass from across the amphitheatre will not be surprised to know that the climb to it is aided. But to reach the aid, you must negotiate a difficult path through boulders and scree. From the pass a steep, aided section drops down to easier ground, but the day's difficulties are not over yet, as a further

exposed, but well-aided, section follows. Now the way undulates, but is always dropping. From the low point a climb of about 800ft (250m) brings you to the Altopiano delle Pale di San Martino, a magnificent Dolomite plateau. Close by, and very welcome after the tough day, is Rifugio Rosetta (8,466ft/2,581m – also called the Giovanni Pedrotti).

From the *rifugio* the top station of the cable car from San Martino di Castrozza is visible, with Cima Rosetta rising behind it. The peak is well worth climbing for a fine view of Cimon della Pala down to the town, a string of fine, jagged peaks and the *altopiano*. The plateau is extraordinary: high, sloping upwards from the west and essentially smooth, though wind, water and time have chiselled away at it. It was once the sea bed of a lagoon, and the surrounding peaks the remains of an atoll. At first glance, and even on cursory inspection, the plateau is barren and desolate, but a closer look reveals patches of alpine plants clinging to life in sheltered nooks and crannies. If time allows, be sure to investigate this most singular of landscapes.

AV2 continues by descending a trench in the plateau, gently at first and then steeply on a zizzagging path carved into the cliff. Then it climbs, with one long aided section, to Passo del Ball (8,013ft/2,443m) before heading easily down to Rifugio Pradidali. Having descended below the west flank of Cima Pradidali, the route now moves below the east flank, passing a shaded lake and then bearing east to Passo delle Lede, from which a steep descent reaches easier ground littered with the debris from a US Air Force plane which crashed in 1957. AV2 continues on, eventually through conifers to Rifugio Treviso, from where it crosses one last high ridge (at Forcella d'Oltro, 7,311ft/2,229m) before descending into a more pastoral landscape to reach Passo Cereda (4,464ft/1,361m).

You are now entering the final stage of AV2, at the extreme southern end of the Dolomites. Though less spectacular than the northern stages, the country here is just as rugged, a wild, arid and much less populated area. In consequence there are fewer opportunities for accommodation, necessitating careful organization if you are not carrying a tent. You should also keep an eye on the weather. Because of its position, this final Dolomite bastion is the first to be swept by warm, often damper air emanating from the low-lying

LEFT The Civetta from Passo Valles.
BELOW The path to Passo delle Farangole.

OPPOSITE Rifugio Pedrotti and the Pale di San Martino from Cima Rosetta.

LEFT Passo di Ball between Cima di Val Roda (right) and Cima Pradidali (left). The pass is named for John Ball (1818–89), the English mountaineer.
BELOW Cima Pradidali (right) and Cima Ball from the high San Martino plateau.

Po valley, which slices its way right across Italy, from the Alps to the Adriatic. That position brings wetter and, crucially, more unstable weather. As the final mountain crossing to Feltre takes at least three days and escape can be problematic, it is not unusual for walkers to decide that Passo Cereda is a suitable end point to AV2.

Those who continue should aim first for Bivacco Feltre, a pair of corrugated huts reached after a short descent to the hamlet of Matiuz and a long, hard climb over difficult ground, occasionally aided, below Piz di Sagron (8,154ft/2,486m) to the Passo del Comedon (6,780ft/2,067m). The *bivacco* has no guardian and no cooker, so you must have the means to cook as well as food and drink; there are, though, good bunks. The walk south is no easier, with difficult ground, but through a beautiful landscape, occasional caves offering primitive shelter if needed. The destination is Rifugio Boz which, if willing to put in an eight-hour day, you can reach from Passo Cereda, ignoring the *bivacco*. The *rifugio* offers good, basic meals as well as accommodation.

Another long day is now needed to reach Rifugio dal Piaz. Cross Passo di Fenestra (5,792ft/1,766m) and then follow a wire-strung ledge carved into the cliff, another reminder of the First World War when the area was again the front line between Italy and Austria: there are several tunnels locally which pierce the ridge. Engineered steps and a cable now aid ascent of Sasso Scarnia (7,301ft/2,226m), though you need not go to the summit – a worthwhile viewpoint – as a rugged path outflanks it to the south. You descend to reach a military mule track that leads into the Belluno Dolomites National Park.

The going is easier now, and you will soon reach Rifugio dal Piaz (6,537ft/1,993m). From here the old military road descends to Passo di Croce d'Aune, from where Feltre, the terminal town, is best reached by bus. In the town, the cathedral is an impressive building with several fine artworks. Elsewhere, there are a couple of interesting old buildings, but Feltre has had an unhappy history which has destroyed much of the old centre. In the early sixteenth century the town was severely damaged in a battle to re-establish the Venetian Republic, then in the late eighteenth century it became French briefly after Napoleon's Italian campaign. It was ceded to Austria, and became Italian in 1866, only to be besieged by the Austrians during the First World War. Aspects of the town's history are explored at the museum in Via Lorenzo Luzzo.

Travel

By air/rail Bressanone is connected by rail to Innsbruck and Verona. The latter is connected to Venice and Bergamo. Bergamo, Innsbruck and Venice all have airports used by low-cost carriers. Feltre also has a rail link to Venice.

By road Bressanone is easily reached by road, being an exit from the A22 autostrada, which crosses the Brenner Pass. The SS50 from Feltre offers a straightforward way of reaching Belluno and the A27 autostrada, which has an exit at Venice airport.

Maps and guides

Treks in the Dolomites, Martin Collins and Gillian Price, Cicerone. This is a fine guide to both *alta vie*.

The best maps are the 1:25,000 series from Tabacco, which cover AV2 on five sheets (north to south): 30, 05 (or 07), 15, 22 and 23. Both Tabacco and Kompass produce 1:50,000 maps which cover the route. However, given the mountainous nature of the route the larger-scale maps are preferable.

Waymarking

In general excellent throughout, though in poor weather in some areas walkers might wish for a few more of the standard red and white paint splashes. As well as the paint splashes there are more conventional signposts, usually at the *rifugi*. These usually indicate the local path number (given on the maps), but often also include 'AV2', which is also occasionally painted into a triangle at strategic points.

Accommodation

Almost all walkers complete AV2 using *rifugi*. Only on the final section into Feltre are cooking equipment, food other than day snacks and even bivouac equipment or tent required, and even then good planning and weather can avoid their use. Escape to upmarket hotels is possible all along the way – particularly to the famous ski area of Val Gardena, to Canazei from Passo Pordoi and to San Martino di Castrozza.

Equipment

In summer it is possible to walk the entire route in shorts and T-shirt, but it would be foolish when crossing terrain that rises towards 10,000ft (3,000m) to be unprepared for cold, wind and rain. Good footwear is also essential, as the ground underfoot is usually rock or rock debris.

Climate

To the mountain walker, the Dolomite climate is enviable, with warm summers and cold winters. Summer temperatures can be high – rather too high perhaps for walkers from northern Europe, and with an accompanying haze which may limit the view. But, as always, mountains can generate local weather so that summer storms can occur suddenly, but clear just as quickly. Be prepared for the unexpected.

Hazards

Hot weather may be a problem. As in all mountain areas you should always keep an eye on the weather and be aware of escape routes on the highest route sections. Though never very remote, AV2 is occasionally remote enough for minor accidents to become serious. In the event of an accident, make contact with the nearest refuge and ask for help.

National Parks and Wildlife

The Puez–Odle Nature Park, extended in 1999 to cover a total of over 25,000 acres (10,000ha), is interesting geologically, particularly for its fossils, and also to botanists and animal lovers. Plant lovers have been entranced by the area ever since Reginald Farrar wrote his famous book *The Dolomites* in 1913, which extolled the virtues of an area where 'every day you could have a different ramble over acres of Geum, Gentian, and Anemone in every direction' and spring was 'a spectacle of bewildering beauty, [with] waving sheets of colour to the horizon'. It is still much as it was when Farrar went.

For the animal lover there are red deer, while bird lovers will see black redstart, alpine chough and snowfinch, while hoping, too, to spot golden eagle or even an eagle owl.

The high plateau of Pale di San Martino is also part of a nature park. Although the major part of the park covers the woodland surrounding the massif, the plateau's alpine flora is a highlight.

At its southern end, AV2 passes through the western edge of the Belluno Dolomites National Park, which covers about 120 sq. miles (300 sq. km) of country north and west of the SS50 which runs towards Langarone from Feltre. Within the park over 110 species of bird have been identified, as well as 100 butterfly species. More unusual birds include wallcreeper, Tengmalm's owl and hoopoe. There are good numbers of chamois, roe and red deer, marmot and mouflon. The area is particularly good for plant life, over 1,400 species having been identified (about 25 per cent of the total for Italy as a whole). Unusual species include silver geranium, which grows only above about 5,500ft (1,700m), and the beautiful carnic lily, another high-altitude plant. There is an information centre for the park at Croce d'Aune.

TOP LEFT German gentian.
ABOVE Rhaetian poppy.
TOP RIGHT Monkshood.
RIGHT Trumpet gentian.

OPPOSITE
LEFT Chamois.
RIGHT Snowfinches. An illustration from a nineteenth century European bird guide.

The Brenta Dolomites

ITALY

Defining the 'best' walk is, of course, always a matter of personal choice. In the Dolomites the traverse of the Sella, described on page 155, would, if not top, certainly come close to the top of most walkers' list. But another contender is the Brenta, that fine Dolomitic outlier which rises above the fashionable ski resort of Madonna di Campiglio.

The Brenta is long (north–south) and narrow (east–west), best explored by walks which take several days. Its rock towers are also steep and angular, apparently constructed for the benefit of the rock climber and the *via ferrata* enthusiast. But the walker wishing to sample its delights can find fine walks, though these usually entail an out-and-back journey if a long climb or descent is to be avoided. Here we explore one such journey.

It begins at the roadside car park at the base of the cable car which rises to a top station near Passo del Grostè (7,977ft/2,432m). Take an early car if you intend the longer day suggested here; those intending a more leisurely walk should remember that the cable car stops for lunch from 1.00 to 2.00 p.m. From the top station signposts indicate Path 316 to Rifugio Tuckett e Sella. On this western edge of the

Brenta the rock forms a high plateau, somewhat akin to the Sella or Pale of AV2, but long and narrow, in keeping with the overall mass. It could sometimes be easy to become lost here, but the route is well signed. The painted arrows on the rocks occasionally bend to indicate a change in direction or a step up to a higher ledge. Mostly, though, the route is easy to follow, tracing a route across the grey rock landscape, with occasional splashes of colour from alpine flowers, and magnificent views right (west) to the peaks of the Adamello, and left (east) to Cima Grostè (9,515ft/2,901m) and neighbouring peaks, and the glacier below them.

OPPOSITE Lunchtime, Rifugio Tuckett e Sella. Above the diners, cloud fills Bocca di Tuckett.

BELOW The walk starts with fine views towards the Madonna di Campiglio valley and, beyond, the Adamello.

RIGHT Francis Fox Tuckett (1834–1913) was one of the foremost British mountaineers of the Golden Age of Alpinism. With Douglas Freshfield and Chamonix guide François Devouassoud, he climbed the Cima Brenta, then thought to be the highest Brenta summit.

BELOW The Val Brenta from near Rifugio Brentei. The peak to the left is the Cima Tosa, the highest Brenta peak.

Ahead the tower and castle of Vallesinella dominate the view as the path undulates towards them. There are occasional descents and climbs, but these are minor, the route being essentially flat. Finally, the Vallesinella, dropping down to Madonna, opens up to the west, and the cableway which supplies the *rifugi* comes into view. It is now just a short step around the commanding rock wall of the Castelletto di Vallesinella Inferiore (8,203ft/2,501m) to the *rifugi* (7,452ft/2,272m), just beyond a little chapel. The first of the two buildings which comprise the *rifugi* was built in 1906 and named in honour of Quintino Sella (1827–84), a scientist turned statesman who, as a finance minister, was responsible for putting Italy on a sound financial footing at a time of extreme political upheaval. A committed alpinist, he also founded the Italian Alpine Club. The second, later, building, was named for Francis Fox Tuckett.

From the huts, follow Path 328 westwards through a jumble of huge boulders and then down to Sella del Fridolin (7,029ft/2,143m), an easily missed shallow pass. Beyond, the route descends a curious, inclined limestone pavement where the aromatic dwarf mountain pine and alpenrose offer the occasional useful handhold. At the base of the pavement there is a path junction. To the right here Path 318 descends easily to Rifugio Casinei, from where you can descend along Path 317 to Rifugio Vallesinella and on down to Madonna. A left turn follows Path 318 into the magnificent Val Brenta Alta, at the head of which Cima Tosa (10,407ft/3,173m) is the highest Brenta peak.

You must now make a decision. Strong walkers can continue, making their way through a tunnel and on to Rifugio Maria e Alberto al Brentei, where a quick coffee and bite to eat will be all there is time for if you are to reach the last Grostè cable car. Those descending directly to Madonna will not need to be in such a hurry. Slower walkers may settle for this view of the Alta valley before returning to Rifugio Sella e Tuckett and on to Grostè. A fine alternative is to spend the night at the Rifugio Brentei, perhaps exploring further in the morning – even far enough along the increasingly difficult Path 318 towards Rifugio Pedrotti to catch a glimpse of the famous Campanile Basso. But that is hardly a day walk . . .

Walk information

Map Kompass 1:25,000 sheet 688. Start/finish: The Grostè cable car base station.
To Rifugio Sella e Tuckett and return Length: 5 miles (8km). Ascent: 350ft (100m).
To Rifugio Brentei and return Length: 9½ miles (15km). Ascent: 850ft (260m).
To Rifugio Sella e Tuckett and descent to Madonna Length: 7½ miles (12km). Ascent: 175ft (50m), but with 2,600ft (800m) of descent.

ABOVE Rifugio Tuckett e Sella beneath Castelletto Inferiore.
LEFT On the walk below the peaks near Cima Grostè.

171

The
Ridgeway

ENGLAND

From eastern Wiltshire a band of chalk downland sweeps north-east across southern England. The downland never reaches the 1,000ft contour (about 305m), so even its highest point does not acquire the status of a mountain. The landscape is not angular or jagged in the way that mountains are. Nor is it wild or rugged. Yet the high scarp on its northern side dominates the area and its history.

The walks in this book seek out wild, invariably mountainous areas, exploring spectacular scenery. In England and Wales, these criteria would direct the walker to the Pennine Way, or perhaps to the Offa's Dyke Path. But landscape can also offer more than wonderful views. The Ridgeway represents one of the most important historical landscapes in Britain, and the landscape of softer, rolling, pastoral chalk downland it traverses has its own charms, making an exploration of this most ancient pathway a delight.

The Ridgeway was designated a National Trail in 1973, but that designation applied to the near 90 mile (about 135km) path from Overton Hill to Ivinghoe Beacon. It can be argued that the true Ridgeway is only the chalk downland that links the prehistoric 'capital' of Britain to the Thames Valley, a distance of about 47 miles (75km), involving no more than 2,000ft (600m) of climbing. Here, although the continuation of the National Trail beyond the Thames is mentioned, that initial journey is the main consideration.

The chalk downland of southern England forms a belt that curves inland from Dorset and then seaward again to end at Dover's White Cliffs. It was formed 65–100 million years ago when a warm sea covered the land: the chalk, an extremely pure form of calcium carbonate, originated from the skeletal remains of sea creatures falling to the seabed, probably augmented by a soup of planktonic material. Later geological movements tilted the chalk band, creating the classic steep scarp slope/gradual dip slope topography we see today. The chalk was formed in three distinct layers, the lowest having a relatively high clay content which forms an effective 'damp proof course', so that water percolating vertically down through the porous chalk is diverted horizontally to emerge as springs near the base of the scarp.

Within the chalk are nodules of flint: hard, lustrous chunks of silicon dioxide believed to have been formed from the remains of silica-rich organisms such as sponges, though the exact mechanism for producing the discrete masses within the chalk matrix is not well understood. Flint can be knapped (struck with a stone to break off flakes) to create sharp edges, a fact that made the area prized by Neolithic folk. There were trees on the downland, but the thin, poor, dry soil meant fewer, sparser trees, which meant that the higher ground was also a safer place than the heavily forested lowlands where dangerous animals lurked. The uplands were also valued because the sandstone laid down on the chalk 25–65 million years ago had been eroded and broken, so that they were covered with blocks of harder stone.

Now called sarsens, these sandstone blocks were ideal for the construction of the megalithic structures that are such a feature of this area of Wiltshire that it has been called the prehistoric capital of Britain. Of those structures the most famous is Stonehenge, which lies a short distance south of the National Trail. But to the archaeologist, Avebury and the nearby megalithic structures are, in many ways, the more impressive. And not only to archaeologists: Charles II, on viewing the site in 1663, maintained, 'It does as much exceed in greatness the so renowned Stonehenge as a cathedral doth a parish church.'

To the argument that the true Ridgeway ends at the Thames can be added an equally compelling one that it should start at Avebury. And that is where we shall start here.

Prehistoric Avebury dates from the Neolithic (New Stone Age) period, usually dated to about 5500–4000 years ago. It began as a circular ditch/bank, built about 4700 BP, later changes and the raising of the stones taking about 500 years. The site is huge, covering 28 acres (over 11ha). The stone circle is surrounded by a ditch 1,140ft (350m) in diameter and up to 30ft (9m) deep, with a bank 4,500ft long and almost 20ft (6m) high. There were about 250 stones, the largest 21ft (6.5m) high and weighing 60 tons. Within the great circle are two

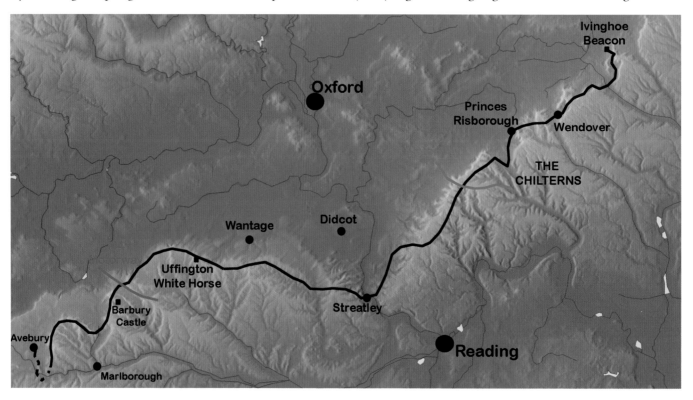

ABOVE The Avebury stone circle.
RIGHT The Avenue.

ABOVE West Kennett long barrow.

LEFT The interior of West Kennett long barrow.

BELOW Silbury Hill.

The Ridgeway on the Marlborough Downs.

smaller circles. Some of the stones are now missing, as the pagan nature of the site persuaded medieval church authorities to regularly overturn, and break up, a stone as an act of faith.

From the circle, an avenue of stones, deliberately chosen as columnar or triangular, suggesting a fertility basis for selection, led south-east towards the Sanctuary (which we visit later), a distance of 1.5 miles (2km). There is also evidence of another avenue heading west. The sheer effort of digging the ditch and raising the bank and stones when the premier tools were antler picks and shovels almost defies belief. Exactly why the stones were erected remains a mystery.

From Avebury you can follow the remaining avenue of stones. At its end, bear right on a permissive path towards Silbury Hill, which can be circumnavigated by path to reach the main A4. Silbury Hill is, in many ways, even more enigmatic than Avebury. The mound is 130ft (40m) and 525ft (160m) in diameter, and required the moving of 14 million cubic feet (400,000 cubic metres) of material. The construction method is understood – a series of circular chalk walls were built, of decreasing diameter as the hill rose, and then filled with rubble – but why was the mound built? It dates from the start of the early phase of Avebury construction (and so pre-dates Egypt's pyramids) and despite numerous efforts, nothing has ever been found within it.

Now cross the A4 and follow its verge, with care, until you come to a signed path, right, leading to West Kennett long barrow, which pre-dates Avebury. This is a typical Neolithic tomb, burial chambers of stone slabs being earthed over to form a 'barrow' 305ft (93m) long, of which the chambers occupy only 40ft (12m). But though typical in

style, West Kennett is far from typical in size; the 'blocking stones' – perhaps barring the entrance to evil spirits, or preventing the spirits of the dead from exiting – are vast. At a time when Neolithic folk had yet to alter the landscape by intensive farming, such barrows, placed in prominent positions, were a statement, and probably represent the tombs of tribal leaders. When excavated, the barrow revealed the skeletal remains of forty-six people.

From the barrow reverse the walk to the bottom of the hill, and then turn right following a path over a track and on to a minor road. Cross and continue to the Sanctuary, where a series of low concrete posts mark the position of wooden posts erected about 5000 BP. The posts probably supported a roof, but again the site remains shrouded in mystery.

The Ridgeway National Trail starts across the main road from the Sanctuary, taking a broad track gently uphill. To the right is Fyfield Down, which is littered with the sarsen stones from which Avebury was constructed. On Hackpen Hill one of Wiltshire's many chalk-cut white horses can be seen; it dates from the coronation of Queen Victoria in 1838. Beyond the horse, the path continues to Barbury Castle.

The castle is actually an Iron Age (i.e. Celtic) hillfort. Such sites were defensive, the local population retreating to it if danger threatened, though there is evidence in many such hillforts of huts, suggesting that some, at least, were permanently or semi-permanently occupied. There is evidence of huts here, but the lack of water would have been a problem for occupiers. Hillforts use ditches and ramparts to enhance the natural contours of the land to create a defence. At Barbury there are two concentric rings of ditch/rampart, suggesting

ABOVE Spring, Barbury Castle.
LEFT Winter, Liddington Castle.

OPPOSITE Wayland's Smithy.

construction in the late Iron Age, after the development of the sling shot, which forced builders to add ditches to keep attackers further back. The enclosed area is about 11 acres (about 4.5ha). Barbury's name probably derives from Beran Byrg, Bera's Hill. Bera may have been a Saxon warlord, as it is known that a Saxon army defeated the Celts near by in AD 556. (The chief of the Saxons was Cynric, but perhaps Bera captured the hillfort or made some other significant contribution.) In the area around the castle there are several round barrows (Bronze Age burial mounds) and flint quarries.

The 'castle' is now the centrepiece of a local Country Park and Nature Reserve: head through the car park etc. and continue along Smeathe's Ridge, a fine section of the trail with extensive views northward. Now descend towards Ogbourne St George, a pretty village, continuing to the hamlet of Southend and the main A436 road.

Across the road – take care crossing, as vehicles travel at speed on this stretch – the trail heads north, parallel to the main road, to reach a point close to Liddington Castle. This is the highest the trail reaches, at about 902ft (275m). The castle – the triangulation point on which is at 909ft (277m) – is not on the route, but worth a detour. It is another hillfort, but usually much less popular than Barbury. Liddington has a single ditch and rampart, and has been suggested as a site for one of the major battles of British history. After the Saxons had settled in south-east England, arriving initially as mercenaries for a Celtic king, they began a push westward to establish Saxon rule throughout the country. At some stage the advance was halted by Celtic armies under King Arthur – the real man, not the legendary figure of the Round Table and the chivalrous band of knights. In about AD 800 the Welsh chronicler Nennius noted that Arthur had halted the Saxon advance in a series of battles which culminated in a major victory at Mons Badonicus, Badon Hill, the location of which has been discussed ever since.

Many historians favour a site on the Ridgeway (though some of the battles listed by Nennius were in northern England), arguing that the Saxons probably used the Thames, ships offering a chance to bypass difficult valley country, but would then likely have used the ancient downland track, a fact borne out, it seems, by the battle close to Barbury Castle. But other sites have been suggested, including Liddington Castle which lies close to the village of Baydon.

From Liddington, where you can tread turf once walked by Arthur, the trail uses a minor road to cross the busy M4 motorway, and then follows an easy track to Wayland's Smithy, another fine Neolithic long barrow. Wayland was the blacksmith of Norse mythology; the name arose from a local legend that a horse left at the barrow overnight, with a coin placed on one of the sarsen blocking stones, would be newly shod next day. Ahead now the trail rises to Uffington Castle, another hillfort, with a single ditch and rampart. There are several burial mounds from the Neolithic and Bronze Ages, but by far the most famous feature is the white horse carved on the hill's northern slope.

The horse is about 360ft (110m) long and 125ft (38.5m) tall, and highly stylized, almost modern abstract in form. It is first mentioned in the twelfth century, which led historians to consider, at first, that it may have been Saxon in origin, perhaps carved to commemorate a victory over Norse invaders. Such a date would also tie in neatly with the naming of Wayland's Smithy, as in Norse tales Wayland rode a white horse. However, recent excavations of the base of the trenches which delineate the figure – rather than being cut in the turf, the figure was trenched and the trenches chalk-rubble filled – have suggested that the first cutting was 3,000 years ago (late Bronze/early Iron Age). As the figure becomes obscured in as little as seven years, the fact that it still exists means that it has received care and attention over more than a hundred generations. Why, in that case, did the locals persist in regular cleaning even when wars raged and the population

changed from Celtic to Saxon, perhaps even Norse? These questions, coupled with the fact that the horse, which is on a thirty-degree slope and so can be seen fully only from the air, have led to many fanciful suggestions involving aliens etc. Whatever the truth, what is clear is that the artist, unable to see his creation from above, was wonderfully skilled.

Below the horse is a flat-topped isolated hillock, an outlier of the down, now separated from the main mass by differential erosion, known as Dragon Hill. Legend has it that it was here St George slew the dragon and the dragon's blood poisoned the soil, so that grass will no longer grow on the hillock's plateau. To the west of the hillock, the lush valley is known as the Manger. Another legend claims that on one night each year the white horse leaves the hillside to graze in the valley, always returning by dawn. The ripples in the valley floor resulted from snow melt at the end of the last Ice Age.

East of Uffington, the trail hugs the scarp edge. To the south here are the Lambourn Downs, famous for racehorse gallops, though the gallops are not visible without detouring. The trail continues east to reach the Devil's Punchbowl, a sweeping incut of the downland, and then passes another hillfort (Segsbury Camp, also called Letcombe Castle, on Castle Hill) before you cross the main A338 road, with care, to reach the Wantage Memorial and a view of the town of the same name. The memorial commemorates Robert Loyd-Lindsay (1832–1901), who was a Brigadier-General in the British army and was awarded the Victoria Cross for bravery during the Crimean War. After his military service he became MP for Wantage and as a philanthropist did much to develop the town.

Close to the memorial, a short distance north, is a section of Grim's Ditch, other, longer sections being visible further along the route near where it reaches the main A34. The feature was named by the Saxons for their god Grim (another name for Woden), synonymous with the Norse Odin. The ditch actually pre-dates the naming by many centuries, the Saxons being fond of assuming supernatural manufacture of impressive features they did not understand. It is now believed the ditch was cut by Iron Age folk in about 300 BC, though why is a

puzzle. To see the ditch – or, rather, its line, as it is now largely filled and traceable only by the trees/hedges that flourish along it – branch left off the trail on Bury Down: the ditch lies close to the base of the scarp. From the same point there is also a view over Harwell Laboratory and across to Didcot Power Station.

The latter is an example of an old technology, burning coal to produce electricity, though Didcot is actually a relatively new station, originally constructed in the late 1960s, but with a newer CCGT station built in the 1990s. With concerns over fossil-fuel burning and the impact of consequent increases in carbon dioxide levels in the atmosphere, the Didcot plant is now seen as an industrial dinosaur. Strangely, the Harwell site was initially seen as heralding a new, nuclear age. However, nuclear power generation became seen as a cul-de-sac, only for global warming to raise its profile again. Much of the Harwell site is now given over to non-nuclear work.

The Ridgeway uses a dispiriting tunnel beneath the main A34 to progress to another downland area used for the training of racehorses. Shortly after emerging from the tunnel, look out for a memorial stone to the left (north) for a young army officer killed in a training accident. Beyond the gallops area, the trail begins a descent into the Thames valley, passing Streatley Warren. The name probably derives from the medieval practice of creating artificial warrens for rabbits, used to supplement the low-meat diet of the locals. Today the warren, which is off the trail and has restricted access during the bird breeding season, is a Site of Special Scientific Interest, set up to protect plant life and birds. Beyond the warren the trail descends to a minor road which it follows into Streatley, a village beside the River Thames.

ABOVE The path to Uffington Castle.

OPPOSITE
ABOVE Uffington White Horse.
BELOW The Vale of White Horse from the top of the chalk figure. The scarred hillock below the figure is Dragon Hill, while the shallow valley to the left is the Manger.

LEFT On the way to the Wantage Memorial.
BELOW The Wantage Memorial.

OPPOSITE
ABOVE From the Ridgeway on the Chilton Downs, the view north extends over the 'modern' complex of Harwell, formerly a centre for nuclear research, and the 'old-fashioned' architecture of the coal-fired power station at Didcot.
BELOW The Thames at Streatley.

THE RIDGEWAY CONTINUATION

From Streatley the Ridgeway National Trail crosses the Thames to Goring, a pretty village, and then follows the Thames upstream towards Wallingford, before turning east, away from the river and traversing the fine beech woodland of the Chilterns. The continuation passes Watlington, crosses the M40 motorway and continues to Princes Risborough, the name of which reflects one-time ownership by Edward, the Black Prince (distinguishing the town from nearby Monks Risborough, which was owned by the monks of Canterbury). Next the trail passes Chequers, the country retreat of the Prime Minister; it then goes through Wendover. After crossing the A41 trunk road and the Grand Union Canal, it turns north to reach Ivinghoe Beacon, from where there is a fine view of the Chilterns, Dunstable Downs and the Bedfordshire plain.

RIGHT Bluebells and beechwoods are a feature of the Ridgeway continuation path. The beeches (FAR RIGHT) are at Burnham.

BELOW Looking north over Aylesbury Vale from Ivinghoe Beacon, the endpoint of the continuation path.

Travel

By air The way lies close to both Heathrow and Gatwick, as well as the provinical airport at Bristol.

By rail The nearest railway station to the start of the walk is Swindon, from where buses travel to Avebury, the start point suggested here, and to Marlborough, with a stop close to Overton Hill, the official start point. Goring, across the Thames from the finish at Streatley, has a rail link to London.

By road Both Avebury and Streatley are served by good roads, and each is on local bus routes.

Maps and guides

The Ridgeway, Nick Hill, Trailblazer Publications.
An excellent guide (covering the whole route, from Overton Hill to Ivinghoe Beacon).

So good is the route marked on the ground that two Ordnance Survey 1:50,000 sheets (173 and 174) are all that is required (with 165 and 175 covering the continuation route). However, the Explorer series (1:25,000) maps are so useful for exploring off the route that they are worth the extra cost and weight of paper. You will need sheets 157 and 170, and for the continuation route Explorer sheets 171 and 181.

Waymarking

Excellent throughout, though the route is so obvious along much of its length that the signposts are a bonus rather than a necessity. On signs that indicate local paths, look for the acorn motif, which is common to all National Trails.

Accommodation

Despite never being far from habitation, the Ridgeway traverses only one hamlet, Southend, near Ogbourne St George. However, there are places only a short distance from the route, and these will have accommodation ranging from bed-and-breakfast stops to quality hotels. Technically camping is not allowed along the route unless the permission of the relevant landowner has been sought. In reality careful campers who camp late and leave early, do not start fires and, most importantly, leave no trace of their stay are unlikely to encounter a problem.

Equipment

The Ridgeway is a low-level route, but it is open and, therefore, weather-swept. Wet-weather gear is therefore essential. Good boots are also important, especially if there has been heavy rain in the period before you start out, as the chalk soil rapidly turns to a glue-like mud that can make sections of the path a trial. That said, in summer after a period of dry weather the going is easy, and only lightweight clothing is needed.

Climate

Southern Britain has warm, often damp summers and cool (rarely cold) damp winters. Each season has its delights on the trail – spring has the flowers, summer the long, balmy days, autumn the best colours, and winter a low light that enhances an otherwise bleak landscape.

Hazards

Until a few years ago the major hazard was the lack of water, which meant walkers had to carry considerable quantities. Recently several taps have been set up – a real bonus to thirsty walkers. The suggested guide has details of their position. Despite protests from walking groups, the Ridgeway, which is technically a byway, still has sections that are open to motor vehicles. The sections are few in number, but amount to about a third of the trail from Overton Hill to Streatley. 4x4s are rarely seen, but motorcycles are more numerous. You will doubtless hear them before seeing them, but be careful. Motorcyclists also make a mess of the path, deep ruts being a particular problem during/after rain. Some walkers see the cyclists and horse riders who are also allowed on the route as a hazard too. In practice horse riders are few in number, as exposed flint can damage hooves, and most cyclists are – like most walkers – well behaved.

Common spotted orchid.

Wildlife

The Nature Reserve at Barbury Castle was set up to protect unimproved chalk downland rich in wild flowers. Look out for cowslip, harebell and the more unusual yellow rattle. Plants at Streatley Warren include the rare early gentian. This plant is legally protected and must not be picked.

Apart from the rare gentian, the plants listed above may be seen anywhere along the route, as may kidney vetch, small scabious and wild thyme. The rich downland attracts butterflies, with rarities such as chalkhill blue, Adonis blue and white admiral being spotted occasionally among the more common peacock, red admiral, marbled white, ringlet and common blue.

Birds include skylark and meadow lark, lapwing and grey partridge. The introduction of red kites to the Chilterns a few years ago has been highly successful and you will be unlucky not to spot at least one. Mammals include roe deer and hare, while only the extremely unlucky walker will not spot the rabbits which, together with sheep, have kept trees at bay and so maintained the grassland and wild flowers. And where there are rabbits there are, of course, foxes.

ABOVE Roe deer.
LEFT Buttercup and friend.

OPPOSITE
ABOVE LEFT Bathing mute swan.
ABOVE RIGHT Red kite.
BELOW Red fox.

The Snowdon Horseshoe

SNOWDONIA, WALES

Relentlessly sliding over the mountains of what is now the Snowdonia National Park, the ice of the last Ice Age carved the Llanberis Pass, one of the most famous rock-climbing areas in Britain, and sculpted the peaks to form cwms. This Welsh word is now often used to describe the geological feature more correctly called a cirque, a steep-sided, horseshoe-shaped valley. One such horseshoe includes the highest peak of the National Park and of England and Wales, Snowdon, or Yr Wyddfa to give it its correct name, and the walk around it is one of the finest mountain walks in Britain.

The horseshoe walk starts from Pen-y-Pass (1,178ft/359m) at the head of the Llanberis Pass, where a café awaits the returning walker and a pay machine confronts the arriving motorist. Leaving the car park from the gap in its far right wall (as viewed from the entrance), you follow a rugged, engineered path known as the Pig Track. The derivation of the name has exercised walkers for decades – is it because

it leads to Bwlch Moch, the Pass of the Pig? But moch can also mean 'quick', so it could merely be the fastest way to cross the shallow ridge. Perhaps 'Pig' just means 'peak'. To add to the confusion, the Ordnance Survey spells the name 'Pyg', allowing others to believe it derives from Pen-y-Gwryd, the nearby hotel, though as the name pre-dates the hotel that is the least likely explanation.

OPPOSITE Winter on the Crib Goch pinnacles, with the summit of Snowdon beyond.

BELOW Summer on the Crib Goch pinnacles, with early morning mist rising from the valleys. In this shot, Snowdon is above the pinnacles, with Crib-y-ddisgl to the right.

Bwlch Moch overlooks the glacial hollow filled by Llyn Llydaw, with the imposing rock wall of Crib Goch to the right. The route heads up that wall, following scrape and other boot marks on the rock, the only clues to the easiest route. Near the top, the wall steepens. Be careful here, as a slip could lead to a serious fall. Finally you reach the top: the narrow, exposed edge of rock that is the summit of Crib Goch (Red Ridge, 3,027ft/923m).

You now traverse the ridge towards sharp, angular pinnacles that appear to bar the way to further progress. The traverse is exposed, and care is needed, particularly in winter. The pinnacles prove much easier than expected, soon allowing a brief descent to Bwlch Coch (2,814ft/858m). From here the walk continues along a much easier path, climbing the wide ridge to the trig-point summit of Crib-y-ddisgl (3,493ft/1,065m) and then descending easily to Bwlch Glas (3,273ft/998m) and the track of the Snowdon Mountain Railway. The 5-mile (8km) track has a gauge of 2ft 7½in (80cm) and an average gradient of 1:7 (the steepest section being 1:5.5). The track was laid in just thirteen months in the mid-1890s, but the opening day (6 April 1896) was marred by the only fatal accident ever to have occurred on the line, when one of two trains descending from the summit left the track and plunged down the mountain. One passenger, thrown clear of the wreck, died from his injuries. The remaining passengers, and a group of walkers whom the plunging wreckage narrowly missed, survived with minor injuries.

You now follow the track to the summit of Snowdon (3,560ft/1,085m). The Welsh name, Yr Wyddfa (The Grave), recalls a legend that the area was once the home of a giant, Rhita Fawr, who amused himself by cutting off the beards of passers-by, stitching the beards into a cloak which he used to ward off winter chills. When he tried to cut off King Arthur's beard, he had met his match, for the legendary king cut off the giant's head. Over time earth and rock covered the giant's body, and the mountain was formed. From the trig-point summit, on a clear day, the Lake District, the Isle of Man and Ireland's Wicklow Mountains are visible.

Just below the summit is the latest building to adorn the mountain. The first was a hotel built soon after the railway opened. This was replaced in the 1930s by a café/shop designed by Sir Clough Williams-Ellis, whose Italianate village of Portmeirion (about 20 miles/35km or so south of Snowdon) is still much admired by architects and visitors. Sadly the same could not be said of his Snowdon building. Lack of care led to the building becoming increasingly shabby, so that Prince Charles, well known for his comments on things architectural, referred to it as the 'highest slum in Britain'. The building was demolished and on 12 June 2009 a new café/visitor centre, designed to blend into the surroundings, was opened.

From the summit you tackle the least pleasant section of the horseshoe, the steep, loose, knee-jarring descent to Bwlch y Saethau (Pass of the Arrows), at about 2,620ft (800m). In legend it was here that King Arthur and the remaining Knights of the Round Table fought the renegade Mordred. The two men came face to face, each striking a killing blow. Mordred died on the spot, but the wounded Arthur was taken down to the shores of Llyn Llydaw. There Arthur told Sir Bedevere to take his sword, Excalibur, and to throw it into Glaslyn, the brooding lake in the dark hollow below Snowdon. Reluctant to lose the legendary sword, Bedevere hid it and returned to Arthur, but from his description the king knew the knight had not done as he had been told. Finally, Bedevere threw the sword into the lake: an arm rose from the surface, grasped the sword, waved it and disappeared. Now Arthur knew Bedevere was telling the truth. A black boat then crossed Llydaw, piloted by three ladies who took the dying king and retreated across

the lake. When the despairing Bedevere asked what would become of him, Arthur called back that he was going to Avalon, where his wounds would be tended and he would await the call to return and save Britain.

Beyond Bwlch y Saethau the route crosses another pass, Bwlch Ciliau (the Pass of Retreat), over which Mordred's defeated army fled. Now you climb twin-summitted Lliwedd (2,945ft/898m), whose north-facing cliffs were the scene of some of the most important rock climbs of the early years of the twentieth century by such pioneers as George Leigh Mallory, who died on Everest in 1924. From the summits, the path descends, with stunning views of the route, to reach the Miners' Track, used originally by miners extracting copper ore at the Brittania Mine on the far shore of Llyn Llydaw, the lake tinted blue by copper salts leaching into the water. Today the track, wide and well maintained, offers the easiest way to Snowdon's summit. Bearing right, east, along it you return to the start. The pipeline to the right feeds water to a small hydro-electric power station at the base of Cwm Dyli.

Walk information

Map: OS Outdoor Leisure sheet 17. Start/finish: Pen-y-Pass. Length: 7.5 miles (12km). Ascent: 3,300ft (1,000m).

ABOVE Bwlch y Saethau, Bwlch Cilau and Lliwedd from Snowdon.
BELOW The horseshoe photographed from the descent from Lliwedd. Lliwedd is the double-peaked mountain to the left. Snowdon is in the centre, with the ridge line to Crib Goch to the right.

The Edges of Helvellyn

LAKE DISTRICT, ENGLAND

The mountain-building phase that created the Lake District raised the ancient land mass comprising slates and volcanic intrusions into a dome centred on Scafell. This dome created a radial drainage pattern, as water ran off it to form a series of valleys arranged like the spokes of a wheel around the hub of the high dome. The last Ice Age turned the streams into glaciers which ground out the valleys, deepening them and then, as the ice retreated, leaving behind piles of moraine which blocked the valley exits. Water collected in the deep hollows carved out by the glaciers, or behind the moraine dams the glaciers created, and so the English Lake District was formed.

Strangely, despite the name, there is actually only one 'lake' in the Lake District – Bassenthwaite Lake – the rest being 'waters' or 'meres'. The largest of the 'lakes' is Windermere, the next largest Ullswater, which lies in the north-eastern corner of the National Park created to protect the majestic scenery of the entire Lake District. Everyone has a favourite lake, but polls suggest that for many visitors Ullswater is the most beautiful of the lakes, the backdrop of uncompromising peaks adding an extra dimension to views across it.

This Z-shaped lake is a little over 7 miles (12km) long, and about 1 mile (1.6km) across at its widest point. At its deepest it is just over 200ft (60m) deep. Ullswater's name is disputed: most experts suggest it derives from Ulf, a local Norse landowner (neighbouring Thirlmere being believed to be from Thorolf, another Norse chieftain), but others prefer Ullr, a Norse god, or Ulphus, a Saxon chieftain, as the name's source. On 23 July 1955 Donald Campbell piloted his Bluebird K7 jet-propelled hydroplane across Ullswater at 202.32mph (325.53 km/h), the first time the 200mph barrier had been broken by a boat. Twelve years later Campbell was killed on Coniston Water when the boat, fitted with a more powerful engine, somersaulted at more than 300mph (over 500km/h).

West of the southern tip of Ullswater, ice carved magnificent corries from the eastern face of a high mountain ridge. One corrie is flanked

OPPOSITE On Striding Edge.

BELOW Ullswater from early on the walk..

LEFT Striding Edge from near the summit of Helvellyn.
BELOW Swirral Edge, Catstye Cam and Red Tarn from the northern edge of Helvellyn's summit plateau.

OPPOSITE
Skiddaw from Helvellyn.

by sharp ridges and holds a glacially formed lake, Red Tarn. It is those edges that are the basis of the walk described here, one which circumnavigates Red Tarn and reaches the summit of Helvellyn, England's third highest mountain.

At the hamlet of Glenridding village, close to Ullswater's southern tip, a large car park offers a convenient (fee-paying) start to the walk. Use the main road to cross Glenridding Beck, and turn right to follow the lane beside the stream until a signed path to the left allows you to ascend through open woodland, awash with bluebells in spring, with fine views towards Ullswater and Glenridding. Where the path descends (towards Grisedale) beyond the crest of an obvious rise, bear right, uphill, to a wall, following it to an elbow where Helvellyn comes into view. Now bear left on a path which leads to Hole-in-the-Wall, a distinct wall gap at about 2,300ft (700m) where a path from Grisedale comes in.

Ahead now is Striding Edge. Longer, though not as sharp or exposed as the Crib Goch ridge on the Snowdon Horseshoe (see page 188), the Edge shares with its Welsh counterpart the classic features of a glacially carved arête. But though less exposed, the Edge is still a serious undertaking, as a memorial plaque close to the start indicates, marking the spot where a follower of the Patterdale hounds fell to his death in 1858. You can follow the top of the Edge, but many walkers take the less exciting path below the crest on the Red Tarn side. At the far end, the Edge has recently been subject to detours, as the National Park attempts to combat the erosion caused by the many walkers tracing this most beautiful of ridges.

Now climb steeply to Helvellyn's summit. The name probably means 'yellow moor', which seems apt, particularly as the summit is an extensive plateau. So extensive in fact that the mountain is probably the only one in Britain on which an aircraft has been deliberately landed. The idea was that of Sir Sefton Brancker, who wanted to popularize civil aviation. Brancker intended to use Snowdon, which is higher, but turned out to be far too sharp. So he climbed Helvellyn and declared the summit as smooth as a billiard table – and about the same size,

maintained his less-than-enthusiastic pilot, John Leeming. After one aborted attempt (during which children at a local school turned out en masse, convinced Father Christmas was coming early), Leeming and co-pilot Bert Hinkler succeeded in landing on 22 December 1926, much to the consternation of a walker on the summit. Take-off looked likely to prove more difficult than landing, but Leeming solved the problem by flying off the cliff edge and out over Red Tarn.

At the Striding Edge end of the plateau, you pass a second memorial to a death on the hill. This one, from 1805, to Charles Gough, is now eroded, but can just about be made out. Gough, a young Quaker, died of a fall from Striding Edge and his dog stood guard over his master until the skeletal remains were found three months later. Wordsworth and Sir Walter Scott each lauded the faithful dog (who was almost equally skeletal on discovery: it seems miraculous the dog survived at all, and many have questioned the exact nature of the dog's diet) in words.

Helvellyn's summit is a marvellous viewpoint, particularly northwards to the peaks of Skiddaw and Blencathra, but also west towards the high Lakeland peaks. At the far end of the plateau a large cairn marks the start of the descent of Swirral Edge, its rock steps heavily marked by crampons, as the walk is a popular winter excursion. Swirral Edge descends steeply; at the base, avoid the eroded path ahead in favour of completing a proper circuit by climbing Catstye Cam (2,919ft/890m) for a fine view of the Red Tarn corrie. Now descend eastwards to pick up a path that leads down to the Greenside Mine site. Lead and silver were mined here for over a hundred years until the 1960s.

From the mine site, a clear path, with fine views to Ullswater, takes you back to Glenridding village.

Walk information

Map: OS Outdoor Leisure sheet English Lakes: North-East. Start/finish: Glenridding village. Length: 8½ miles (13.5km). Ascent: 3,100ft (950m).

The Kerry Way

IRELAND

Kerry is the most south-westerly county of Ireland and its most scenic, combining mountains, a long section of rugged Atlantic and a host of beautiful lakes. The county is also interesting historically. Called Chiarraí in Irish, it is named for the Cairraighe, a tribe who, legend has it, were led by Cair, a son of Fergus mac Rióch, a king of Ulster in the early years of Christendom. Fergus, a man of legendary size and sexual energy, was the lover of Mdeb, Queen of Connacht (who once adorned the Irish pound note in the days before the country joined the Eurozone). So great a lover was Fergus that it is claimed Mdeb needed thirty men to satisfy her if he was not available. Small wonder, perhaps, that the son of this union was able to father an entire tribe.

If the legendary basis of Kerry's people is fascinating, the reality is no less so, with sites covering the time from prehistory to the present day.

Kerry's mountains include the wonderfully named MacGillicuddy's Reeks, named for a local family who owned the land around the reeks (crests) for many centuries. The mountains (which in Irish are called Na Cru acha Dubha – the Black Stacks) include Carrauntoohil, at 3,952ft (1,040m) the highest peak in Ireland. The peak's evocative name (Corrán Tuathail in Irish) means the sickle of Tuathail, another legendary character.

Given the superb mix of scenery and history it is no surprise that a long-distance path, the Kerry Way, has been threaded through the landscape. The way covers a little over 125 miles (200km), but involves very little climbing, reaching a highest point of just 1,233ft (376m), though crossing several passes at 650–1,000ft (200–300m) and requiring about 15,000ft (4,500m) of climbing in total (if the more demanding of two alternative sections is selected). A drawback of the way is the amount – some 38 per cent – that follows roads or lanes. That is much more than the walker would wish, but the sections of country, both wild and pastoral, that lie beyond those tarmac links make the way very worthwhile.

ABOVE A jaunting car.

OPPOSITE
ABOVE Muckross House.
BELOW Evening light across Muckross Lake and Purple Mountain.

The way starts at the delightful town of Killarney. The town owes its origins to Thomas Brown, the 4th Viscount Kenmare who, in the mid-nineteenth century, developed an existing hamlet into a town and built roads to link it with the rest of the country. The development led rapidly to Killarney becoming Ireland's chief tourist destination, and many of the town's most important buildings date from the period immediately following Kenmare's development. Perhaps the most interesting building is St Mary's, Augustus Pugin's neo-Gothic cathedral. Begun in 1842, building work was halted during the Great Famine of 1845–52. The famine, whose primary cause was potato blight, resulted in the death of a million people and saw the emigration of a million more, reducing the Irish population by some 25 per cent. During the famine, Pugin's half-completed cathedral was used as a shelter/hospital for the sick, work not being completed until 1855. In recent years both Pugin and Gothic Revival architecture have seen their reputations soar, and St Mary's is now considered one of the foremost works of both architect and style.

The official start of the way is the bridge over the River Flesk, south of the town. Beyond, the way soon reaches the border of the Killarney National Park and the shore of Castlelough Bay, a wide inlet of Lough Leane. The lake, at approximately 7.5 sq. miles (19 sq. km), is by a large margin the largest of the three famed Lakes of Killarney. Once heavily polluted by sewage and agricultural run-off, it is now in a much better state. For the visitor to County Kerry the three lakes, formed when the ice tongues of the last Ice Age retreated and water

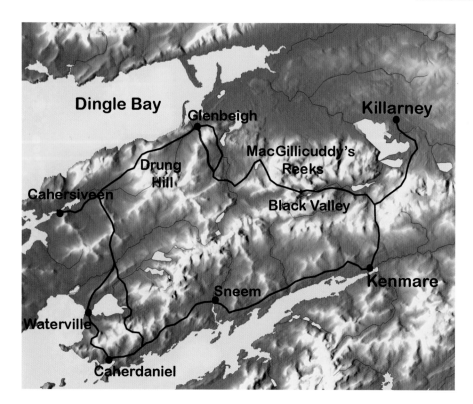

filled ice-scoured rock basins, are a showpiece. At Lough Leane's heart is Innisfallen, an island on which a monastery was built in the seventh century. The monastery was a centre of learning; a story maintains that King Brian Boru, Ireland's most famous ruler, was educated here. Although nothing remains of that first monastery, the ruins of later monastic buildings can still be seen. On a headland jutting into the lake, close to Killarney and just a short detour from the way, stands the beautifully restored fifteenth-century Ross Castle. The waters of Lough Leane are claimed to hide Tir na n'Og, the land of youth where no one ages. One legend tells of Oisin, an Irish warrior, who follows the golden-haired Niamh to Tir na n'Og but, after three years, returns to the land, anxious to see his tribe again, only to discover that Ireland has aged three centuries.

The way soon reaches the second of the three Killarney lakes. Muckross is the deepest of the three, at about 245ft (74m), and is divided from the larger lake by the Muckross Peninsula, a ridge of carboniferous limestone, a remnant of the limestone sheet that once covered the Old Red Sandstone which composes the Kerry hills but has been largely eroded by ice, water, wind and time. As you approach the lake, you pass close to the well-preserved ruins of the fifteenth-century Franciscan Muckross Abbey, and even closer to the Victorian Muckross House. This elegantly furnished house and its beautiful gardens are one of Ireland's most-visited attractions. The

house/gardens complex includes a rural 'museum' (a working 1930s farm), craft workshops and an arboretum. On this section of the way, you will probably also see jaunting cars (two-wheeled, horse-drawn carriages, formerly a local means of transport, but now almost exclusively reserved for tourists).

The way heads south towards Torc Mountain, passing Torc Waterfall, a delightful series of short drops through a fine gorge, and then follows the old Kenmare Road, the main road until the 1830s, climbing through beautiful woodland to reach open land with a view west to MacGillicuddy's Reeks. The descent is through more woodland in Esknamucky Glen, reaching a point that you will recognize some 120 miles (190km) later: the Kerry Way is essentially circular, but begins/ends with a short out-and-back section from/to Killarney.

The way now descends from Galway's Bridge to follow the southern edge of the third Killarney lake, Upper Lake, which is linked to Muckross Lake by the Long Range, a narrow channel which emerges at the Meeting of the Waters at Muckross' far south-western edge. But the lake is only occasionally visible, so dense is the oak and holly woodland. After heavy rain, the lake floods the route close to its western tip, necessitating a pioneering approach to reach Lord Brandon's Cottage. This was the hunting lodge, and one-time home, of the Revd William Crosbie, rector of Castleisland and Baron Brandon. The early nineteenth-century building is now ruinous, but there is a modern café/restaurant at the site.

The way next follows a quiet country lane to Black Valley, soon reaching another lane, to the right, which leads to the Gap of Dunloe, one of the most picturesque local spots. The Gap is a narrow pass

LEFT Early morning in Esknamucky Glen.

ABOVE The route has an out-and-back journey from Killarney to the base of Eskamucky Glen where this signpost will be seen twice by walkers who complete the route. As indicated by the sign, there is a choice: turn left to head for the pass between Peakeen Mountain (right) and Knockanaguish (left) in the photograph BELOW, or turn right towards the Black Valley.

OPPOSITE Black Valley.

between MacGillycuddy's Reeks and Purple Mountain, which, being a difficult drive, is often reached by jaunting car.

Within Black Valley the way follows the road and then an old track, past fields and occasional houses, with the southern flank of the ice-sculpted Old Red Sandstone Reeks to the right and Cummeenduff Lough to the left – a very dramatic section of the walk. When you reach tarmac again, you follow it to soon reach a sign that points towards the old Lack Road, which cleverly climbs through a gap in the hills before descending to Lough Acoose and the inn at Glencar. The way crosses the Caragh River and heads north-west towards the coast, with fine views of Lough Caragh to the right. There is now a choice: a short route climbs through Windy Gap, between Seefin, right, and an outlier of Beenreagh, to reach views of Dingle Bay and Glenbeigh, while a longer, scenic route contours Seefin to reach a fine view of the bay and Caragh Creek.

Glenbeigh lies close to Rossbehy beach, a sandy arm that extends into Dingle Bay, an area of coast associated with another version of the Tir na n'Og legend. In this, Oisin and Niamh ride a white horse into the sea of Dingle Bay to reach Tir na n'Og. Oisin can ride the horse back to his homeland at any time, but Niamh warns him he must not dismount. But on his return, seeing men trying to move a huge stone, Oisin climbs down from the horse to help and instantly ages 300 years.

The way heads south-west from the village, following a section of old railway line and then a minor road to reach the flank of Drung Hill,

from where there are marvellous views across the bay to the Dingle Peninsula. If time permits, it is worth exploring the mountains south of Drung Hill, as the area is one of the most important sites in Ireland for rock art, the geometric motifs dating from the Neolithic and Bronze Ages. The way passes close to these sites, but does not actually reach any of them as it follows tracks and lanes on a descent towards the coast.

For those looking for accommodation or history, the out-and-back detour to Cahersiveen is now worthwhile. You reach this attractive town, set close to the mouth of the Valencia River, after passing an extraordinary sculpture of St Brendan's boat. The saint's journey in the early sixth century, which some claim took him all the way to America, is said to have started close to the town. Cahersiveen was the birthplace of Daniel O'Connell (1775–1847), the Catholic emancipator and campaigner against the union of Britain and Ireland. The town's church is dedicated to him, the only one in Ireland dedicated to a lay person. Those interested in prehistory will find much of interest locally, particularly on Valencia Island (which can be reached by a short ferry ride), where there are many standing stones and ancient tombs. From Cahersiveen, return to the foot of Coomduff Hill.

The way climbs Coomduff Hill, and then climbs south along a fine ridge line to Knockavahaun (1,217ft/371m). Then it descends to follow lanes, tracks and a lower ridge line, through country studded

Beyond Lough Acoose there is a choice of routes. The shortest way follows a path over Windy Gap (LEFT) with a final view of the Reeks, while a longer route bears north-east, rounding Seefin Mountain to reach a magnificent view of Dingle Bay and the Dingle Peninsula (BELOW).

OPPOSITE
ABOVE Commeenduff Glen, which leads to the old Lack Road, the pass beside the Reeks.
BELOW Walkers on the Kerry Way must be prepared for poor weather, as suggested by this photograph taken just after emerging from a low cloud base on the old Lack Road which is followed from the Black Valley to Lough Acoose.

with ancient standing stones, to reach Waterville, a village hemmed in by Ballinskelligs Bay on one side and Lough Currane on the other. This sheltered spot was popular with Charlie Chaplin, whose statue can be seen close to the shore. An alternative route avoids Waterville, branching off on the descent to the town to pass east of Lough Currane, crossing Eagles Hill to rejoin the 'official' route east of Caherdaniel.

From Waterville the 'official' way follows lanes and tracks south, and then turns east around the base of Farraniaragh Mountain, with fine views of the coast. A short variant of the way now goes to Derrynane House, once the home of Daniel O'Connell. Set in 300 acres/120ha of parkland which form the centrepiece of a small National Historic Park, the house, with its memorabilia of O'Connell, is a popular tourist attraction. The variant follows a road, passing an Ogham stone, to reach the tiny village of Caherdaniel.

From Caherdaniel walkers who follow the 'official' route have a fine view of Eagles Hill as they continue eastwards. They will also be able to make out the huge stone wall of Staigue Fort away to the left. Though not on the way, the fort is worth the short detour. The age of Staigue is debated, general opinion favouring a fourth-century AD construction, though dates up to 500 years earlier have been suggested. The builders of this fort and others in the area – the way passes a less impressive one to the west of Caherdaniel – are equally enigmatic, local legend suggesting they were small, and had immigrated to the area in search of copper, which is known to have been mined locally. The immense walls of the fort, still up to 18ft/5.5m high and 13ft/4m thick, including two chambers that have corbelled roofs (similar to those at

the famous Newgrange tomb), show remarkable building skills, as mortar was not used.

Beyond Staigue, the way continues east along tracks and lanes – with a short section of walking beside the main N70: use the wide verge and take care – and reaches Sneem. The town's Irish name is An tSnaidhm,

RIGHT On the coastal alternative, beyond Waterville and Farraniaragh Mountain, the route drops down towards Caherdaniel, passing a large outcrop of fuschia.
BELOW After the coastal and mountain alternatives have rejoined, the route follows a short section of main road before turning off towards Coomcallee Mountain.

OPPOSITE
ABOVE Looking down on Cahersiveen and the Valencia River from the pass beside Drung Hill.
BELOW The statue of St Brendan's boat on the outskirts of Cahersiveen.

which means 'the knot'. The exact reason for the name is disputed – does it refer to the knot-like swirl of water formed where the River Sneem meets the Kenmare River, or to the fact that the town has two squares linked (tied) by a single bridge? The town, with its colourful buildings, is famous for its sculptures, which form an outdoor art gallery, many well-known artists having created works. The panda sculpture was donated by the Chinese government, that of the goddess Isis by the Egyptians. Almost as surprising as these is the statue of General de Gaulle, who often visited Sneem. There is also a statue of Steve 'Crusher' Casey, who was born in Sneem but emigrated to the USA, where he was several times world heavyweight wrestling champion.

There are several short sections of walking beside the N70 to the east of Sneem, the compensation being fine views of the Kenmare River. The main road and the way cross Blackwater Bridge; the way then traverses fine oak woodland before having to follow the N70 for a much longer section before it can escape northwards, climbing to Gortamullin (672ft/205m), from where there are marvellous views south to the Kenmare River and north to the Kerry Mountains. Now the way descends to Kenmare.

The town, named for its position at the head of the Kenmare River estuary – *ceann mhara* means 'head of the sea' – has a long history. It is claimed the Vikings raided here, though even then it was an ancient site; one of Ireland's largest stone circles lies near by. However, the town we see today owes its origins to Sir William Petty, who mapped Ireland for Oliver Cromwell and was granted the area in thanks. Petty laid out the town in the last third of the nineteenth century. In 1861 a convent of the Poor Clare Sisters was founded in the town and the nuns soon became famous for their lace-making. The history of Kenmare lace is explored at the Kenmare Lace Design Centre, where the craft is still practised.

The way leaves the town along a minor road, and then takes the old road to Killarney, a gravel track which climbs between Peakeen Mountain, left, and Knockahaguish, right, to reach a final mountain pass. The view north expands at you reach the pass; and it stays with you as you descend to reach the junction encountered on the outward journey. You now reverse the outward route back to Killarney.

OPPOSITE
ABOVE LEFT The statue of Crusher Casey in Sneem.
ABOVE RIGHT Market Day, Kenmare.
BELOW The Kenmare River from Gortamullin.

BELOW Ruined cottage in Black Valley.

Travel

By air Flights are available to Dublin, Cork and Shannon (near Limerick).

By ferry Walkers wishing to make their way from the UK to County Kerry can use the ferries that link Fishguard to Rosslare, Holyhead to Dublin and Dun Laoghaire, and Liverpool to Dublin.

By rail and road Once you are in Ireland there is a good rail service from Dublin to Killarney, and good road links to Killarney from across the island.

Maps and guides

The Kerry Way, Sandra Bardwell, Rucksack Readers.

Five sheets of OSi (the Irish Ordnance Survey) 1:50,000 Discovery series are required to cover the route – sheets 70, 78, 83, 84 and 85. However, there are only very short sections of the route on sheets 70 (about 2.5 miles/4km) and 85 (about 1.25 miles/2km). It is possible to complete the walk without those sheets, but they have the advantage of enabling you to pick out the peaks of the Dingle Peninsula (sheet 70) and the Shehy Mountains (sheet 85).

Waymarking

The official waymark of the route is a black post with a yellow walker icon. However, in places this is supplemented by yellow arrows on black posts, the icon on rocks and trees (often with accompanying paint splashes) and more elaborate signposts. In general the waymarking is excellent, but there are places where the signs are obscured by vegetation or absent. Map and guide are essential to keep you on route.

Accommodation

There is an abundance of hotels, guesthouses and bed-and-breakfast establishments along the route. There are YHA hostels in the Black Valley and near Killarney. For those wishing to camp, there are several official campsites. All the land crossed by the way is privately owned, so walkers wishing to camp wild must seek permission from the landowner.

Equipment

The route is neither remote nor high, so specialist equipment is not needed. However, County Kerry's position, adjacent to the Atlantic Ocean, means that rain and wind are possible and rain- and wind-proof top-layer clothing is essential.

Climate

County Kerry's position means its climate is dominated by the Atlantic Ocean; the Gulf Stream brings cool summers and warm, damp winters, but the weather is also both unpredictable and changeable. Frosts are uncommon, but rain is not. The well-known name of Ireland, the Emerald Isle, reflects the lushness of its vegetation. But, as has been often noted, the lushness is a reflection of the rainfall: County Kerry sees an average of 220 days annually on which rain falls (though to be fair, a rainy day is defined as one on which at least 1mm of rain falls, and 1mm hardly represents a seriously wet day). Walkers should

therefore expect some rain, but temperatures, even on the warmest days, will not reach those experienced on the walks in southern Europe.

Hazards

The Kerry Way is a low-lying route through populated, rather than remote, country, so although bad weather can be a nuisance it is never a true hazard. The road-walking sections do represent a hazard, as in some places the roads and lanes are narrow and tree-/hedge-lined, so there is limited room for vehicles and walkers. Walkers should use the verges wherever possible and take great care at all times. Midges and horseflies abound in summer.

Official advice on the way is that dog owners should not bring their animals, as much of the route crosses farmland, and dogs worrying farm animals are liable to be shot.

OPPOSITE Red deer calf, near Muckross Lake.

BELOW Pub sign, Kenmare.

National Parks and Wildlife

The Killarney National Park was the first to be established in Ireland. Its 40 sq. miles (102 sq. km) cover the Lakes of Killarney, together with the Purple Mountains, Torc and Mangerton Mountains, and the largest sections of native forest remaining on the island. The park has been designated a UNESCO World Biosphere Reserve.

Of the park's woodlands, the most important are the 4.5 sq. miles (12 sq. km) of native sessile oak in which holly and strawberry trees also thrive. The oak woods are also home to rare lichens and mosses. The purple hairstreak butterfly, whose caterpillars feed exclusively on oak leaves, is found here. The park also has a small forest of yew, which grows on the karst limestone pavement on the Muckross Peninsula. The woodland, known as Reenadinna Wood, is important, as such yew forests are now very rare. Some of the trees are believed to be more than two hundred years old and Reenadinna is home to several rare mosses. The park also has an important area of wet woodland where alder, ash and willow thrive.

The park includes areas of blanket bog and heath, which are extremely important for the growth of rare plant species. The rarest of the park's plants is the Killarney fern, which favours damp places. Once common, it was gathered for sale to tourists to the point where its survival was at stake. Today the places where it still grows are few, their whereabouts kept secret. More common, though still rare, is greater butterwort. Also known as the Kerry violet, this is a carnivorous bogland species that consumes insects to obtain the nitrogen it needs which the nutrient-poor environment does not supply.

Park birds include many woodland species such as redstart and wood warbler. Both chough and nightjar breed here. Upland species include raven and stonechat, and the much rarer ring ouzel and red grouse. Raptors include peregrine falcon and merlin, and in 2007 a programme to reintroduce the white-tailed eagle was begun. There are many waterbird species on the park's lakes; wintering birds include a small number of Greenland white-fronted geese.

Mammals include red squirrel and pine marten, and the only remaining herd of red deer on the island. Sika deer, introduced in the mid-nineteenth century, also breed in the park, and their habit of honing their antlers on yew trees, together with bark stripping, has led to the erection of a deer fence around Reenadinna Wood.

Both within and outside the National Park, plant and bird life is abundant because of the pastoral nature of the county. Look out for foxgloves and cowslips, and also for shamrock (from seamróg – clover). The shamrock is not one species: at various times white clover, red clover, lesser trefoil, black medic and even some wood-sorrels have been claimed as the true shamrock. All are equally unlikely to show the required lucky four leaves. Bird life includes most common northern European species, while on the coast the relatively unusual greater black-backed gull may be seen, as well as the more common herring gull. Visitors who have time to explore the coast should look out for Irish spurge, a tall plant with yellow-green flowers. The plant's fruiting bodies are wart-like, a fact which probably contributed to the idea that the milky sap in the stems was a cure for warts.

LEFT White-tailed eagle.

OPPOSITE
LEFT ABOVE Irish hare.
LEFT CENTRE Giant rhubarb.
LEFT BELOW Devilsbit scabious.
RIGHT ABOVE Irish spurge.
RIGHT CENTRE Silver-spotted Kerry slug.
RIGHT BELOW Greater butterwort.

Diamond Hill

CONNEMARA, IRELAND

Connemara, arguably the most famous of the regions of Eire, is a broad peninsula of land thrust out into the Atlantic Ocean, with sea bordering three sides. The peninsula is dominated by the mountains commonly known as the Twelve Pins (occasionally the Twelve Bens), with peaks to 2,350ft (725m) high and formed from metamorphic rocks. The mountains rise from bogland, a habitat whose importance persuaded the Irish government, in 1980, to create a National Park covering an area of almost 5,000 acres (2,000ha) to the west of Kylemore Lough. The park incorporates several of the Pins, though not the highest peaks.

National Park status, and a collection of high peaks, might seem to indicate an area tailor-made for walkers, but in practice access problems create problems for any writer bold enough to suggest excursions across the high peaks. Add to that the potential for damaging the fragile ecology of the bogs, and erosion problems on some of the hills, and the picture is far more difficult than first imagined. In an effort to forge a path between the desires of walkers and the needs of conservation and good neighbourliness, the park authorities have therefore attempted to persuade walkers to concentrate their efforts on a single peak, Diamond Hill, close to the park's visitor centre. The decision can, of course, be criticized. But many will have sympathy with the park's position, seeing the decision as both pragmatic and, if not ideal, a reasonable way forward. Diamond Hill is a marvellous viewpoint (though the view is, of course, of enticing country as far as walkers are concerned), and the path to it passes through excellent country.

The walk starts at the visitor centre, following a clearly marked path which heads uphill, with engineered sections and an expanding view north across Ballynakill Harbour. To the sides of the path slabs is the

OPPOSITE Ballynakill Harbour from the summit of Diamond Hill.

BELOW Morning light on Kylemore Lough.

bogland that the park seeks to protect. The nutrient-poor soil means that several species of insectivorous plants make a home here, including great and oblong-leaved sundews, and pale butterwort. On higher ground plants more usually associated with colder climes (such as the Arctic) are found, for instance purple saxifrage. The bird life of the park is also impressive, including relatively unusual species such as golden plover, woodcock, wheatear and merlin.

The engineered path eventually runs out below the summit and the final climb is more in keeping with the mountain terrain. From the ridge-like summit there is a view south-east towards the Twelve Pins, and north-east to Kylemore Lake, the smaller lakes to the west of it and the mountains to its north.

From the summit you can complete a circuit of the hill by continuing along the ridge and descending to gain the engineered path, which drops down the north side of the peak and then bears south to regain the outward route. It is now possible to take an alternative route back to the visitor centre by bearing right along a path that runs directly downhill. At the centre there is a café as well as a small exhibition on the flora and fauna of the bog.

Walk information
Map: Ordnance Survey Ireland 1:50,000 sheet 37. Start/finish: The National Park Visitor Centre, near Letterfrack. Length: 3 miles (5km). Ascent: 1,475ft (450m).

All the photographs were taken very early in the curious light of a misty morning, with heavy rain arriving soon after.

RIGHT A Brocken Spectre. Spectres are only produced when low-angle light casts a figure's shadow onto fine mist. Here the spectral halo is a full rainbow of colours.
BELOW Ballynakill Harbour.

OPPOSITE
ABOVE On the approach to Diamond Hill.
BELOW The Twelve Pins from Diamond Hill.

The West Highland Way

SCOTLAND

At first glance, Scotland, particularly the Highlands, would appear to be ideal country for a long-distance path. But 'ideal' is in conflict with 'idea': landowners are suspicious of any plan which, brought to fruition, would involve an increased number of walkers on their land, and many Scots, understandably jealous of their landscape and nervous of what they see as the organized chaos of National Parks and the like, share their lack of enthusiasm. Ultimately, access issues and the needs of conservation saw Scotland, somewhat reluctantly, accept the idea of National Parks, and in the early years of the present century two were established (Loch Lomond and the Trossachs in 2002, and the Cairngorms in 2003). The first long-distance footpath preceded the parks, but the official establishment of the West Highland Way in 1980 still lagged behind the creation of similar National Trails in England. And even in 1980, the opening of the way was not without controversy, the signage, path construction, bridges and other walker-related furniture necessary for an official route being at odds with the idea many people had of Scotland being a wilderness best left to those with the gumption to explore it in the raw. But the Highland Way is now recognized as a magnificent route, threading from an urban landscape to a wild one and, in doing so, exploring Scotland's history as well as some of its scenic highlights.

The route (95 miles/150km, and involving about 8,000ft/2,450m of climbing) begins in Milngavie, a commuter suburb of Glasgow (though the inhabitants would almost certainly disagree with that description). The town name is pronounced 'Mullguy', perplexing many visitors. Most walkers will arrive by train from Glasgow and take a signed underpass to reach the town centre, where a granite obelisk and elaborate archway mark the way's official start.

Despite the urban start, the way very soon reaches open countryside, climbing to a ridge from where you can see the first hills: the pillow lavas of the Kilpatrick Hills to the west, and the Campsie Fells ahead. The route now enters the Mugdock Country Park, an extensive area of wood and parkland around the ruins of the fourteenth-century Mugdock Castle, which was gifted to the people of Scotland by Sir Hugh Fraser in 1980. The route passes the fine Craigallian Loch, and then exits the park and heads towards the first viewpoint of the Highlands: Ben Lomond is visible to the north, beyond the much closer, wooded, volcanic plug of Dumgoyach and shapely, basaltic Dumgoyne. To the right as you descend towards Dumgoyach are five Neolithic standing stones. Ben Lomond has now disappeared from view, the way traversing a pastoral landscape and passing the Glencoyne distillery. It crosses the main A81 twice (be careful) and then follows a minor road towards Drymen. Both John Napier, the mathematician often credited with the invention of logarithms, and George Buchanan, one-time tutor of Mary, Queen of Scots, lived locally, Buchanan having a memorial in nearby Killearn.

The Highlands tempt the walker again soon, Conic Hill above Loch Lomond being visible briefly before a section in the conifer Garadhban Forest shuts out all views until you reach the lower slopes of the hill. You can now climb Conic Hill (1,184ft/361m) for a magnificent view of Loch Lomond and its surrounding hills. (Please note that dogs are not permitted on the approach to Conic Hill during lambing.)

Lomond is a freshwater loch lying on the Highland Boundary Fault, which slices through Scotland from the Isle of Arran to Stonehaven. The fault, active during the Caledonian orogeny (mountain building),

separates older, Pre-Cambrian and Cambrian metamorphic rocks to the north and west from mainly Old Red Sandstone conglomerates to the south and east. Loch Lomond is 24 miles (39km) long and 5 miles (8km) wide at its widest (but only about 0.75 miles/1.25km at its narrowest), and is the largest body of freshwater in Great Britain by surface area. The loch has an average depth of about 120ft (37m), the deepest point being 629ft (190m) below the surface. In terms of freshwater volume, Loch Ness is larger. Though Ness's monster makes it equally famous to the world as a whole, the famous song – with its chorus 'Oh! Ye'll tak the high road, and I'll tak the low road,/And I'll be in Scotland afore ye,/But me and my true love will never meet again,/On the bonnie, bonnie banks o' Loch Lomond' – makes Lomond much the most romantic. The song was reputedly written by a young Scottish prisoner languishing in an English prison after capture in 1745 following the Jacobite rebellion. Having been sentenced to death, he was writing one last letter home and included in it the poem that was later set to music. That legend has been challenged, though most experts agree that the writer was most probably dying away from his beloved Scotland. The chorus refers to a Gaelic tale that the spirit of someone who died away from home was guided back along a 'low

After leaving Mugdock Country Park the route heads for the wooded hillock of Dumgoyach, a volcanic remnant, as is Dumgoyne to the right.

road' prepared by fairies. The 'high road' alternative would have been the journey taken by a returning traveller, a route which would, of course, take much longer.

From Conic Hill the way descends through excellent mixed woodland to the tourist trap of Balmaha, reaching it at the car park beside the National Park Information Centre. Off shore is Inchcailloch, a wooded island; together with the bay to the south, the island forms the Loch Lomond Nature Reserve. From Balmaha the way follows the lakeside road, or paths closer to the shore, to the road end at Rowardennan. The path runs through fine woodland, which is being replanted in places to restore the native form. The oak trees here were originally harvested to provide charcoal for iron smelting. Later, when coal replaced charcoal, the bark was taken for use in the tanning of leather. There is a fine view of Ben Lomond from the road end, and the car park is a favoured starting point for baggers of the most southerly of Scotland's 283 Munros (2009 figure).

The way ignores the top, staying close to the lake on a woodland path that passes Rob Roy's Prison, a shore-side crag. The name is almost certainly fanciful, but Rob Roy MacGregor was a real person. The name 'Roy' was from the Gaelic *ruadh*, red, added to his name

because of his red hair. Born sometime between 1660 and 1671, he lived locally, farming and cattle droving. Threatened with loss of livelihood by either cattle theft or the collapse of his droving, or pursued for debts he owed the Duke of Montrose (accounts vary), Rob Roy turned outlaw, his thefts aimed mainly at Montrose. Eventually he was caught and imprisoned, but he was released to live out a quieter life, dying in 1734 or 1735. His tale was romanticized in a novel by Sir Walter Scott, and then given the Hollywood treatment in a film starring Liam Neeson, with Jessica Lange as the love interest.

The woodland walk continues to Inversnaid, immortalized in a fine poem by Gerard Manley Hopkins. Walkers are welcome at the hotel, but please use the entrance at the back and remove wet gear before going in. Northwards, you can visit another site associated with Rob Roy by scrambling along a side path to reach a cave (thoughtfully marked 'CAVE' by a graffiti artist, who certainly knew a geological feature when he/she saw one). As he was local and an outlaw, it is not beyond belief that Rob Roy did actually use the cave, but it is worth remembering that this was once called King Robert's Cave after a legend that Robert the Bruce was forced to use it during a less successful phase of his career.

At the northern end of Loch Lomond the way exits forest briefly, climbing to open land – there is one last view of Ben Lomond from here and then descends to the tight, wooded valley of the River Falloch. It crosses the river over a bridge a mile or so (about 2km)

ABOVE The Falls of Falloch.
RIGHT Ben Lomond from near Rowardennan. In the distance is Ptarmigan Lodge.

OPPOSITE
ABOVE Evening light over Loch Lomond from Conic Hill.
BELOW The path beside Loch Lomond.

upstream of the Falls of Falloch and passes beneath the main A82 road to reach an old military road.

In Scotland 'old military road' on Ordnance Survey maps instantly suggests the name General Wade. After the Jacobite rebellion of 1715 in support of the Old Pretender, the government in London realized that the coast of northern Scotland had numerous harbours where a sympathetic French army could land, and that armies could form, train and hide in the huge expanse of the Highlands. The government decided that the area must be opened up by the building of roads which would allow relatively speedy access for an army if trouble flared. The Irish-born George Wade (1673–1748), a career soldier who had distinguished himself in service with Marlborough in Spain, was appointed Commander-in-Chief of His Majesty's Northern Army with the job of ensuring access. Starting in 1724 Wade built about 300 miles (480km) of roads and forty bridges, linking the southern lowlands to forts constructed at Inverness (Fort George), Fort Augustus and Fort William. After the 1745 rebellion (in support of Bonnie Prince Charlie, the Young Pretender) the government appointed Major William Caulfield, who had been Wade's surveyor, to continue

the road-building programme. Though Caulfield actually built a greater length of road than Wade, his name is barely known. It is Caulfield's road through Lochaber – realigned by Thomas Telford at one point – that the West Highland Way now follows.

The route bypasses Crianlarich, where the military road from Stirling heading for Fort William met that built from Loch Fyne over the 'Rest and Be Thankful' pass to Loch Lomond. Today, wayfarers detour to the town – whose beautiful name is from the Gaelic for 'low pass' – for rest and refreshment; there is a youth hostel here among other options for accommodation. In the forest west of the town the route reaches its halfway point. It continues through the forest, a mix of conifer and broad-leaf, silver birch and mountain ash (rowan) predominantly, crossing a railway line, the main A82 – take great care, traffic moves quickly here – and the River Fillan to reach the remains of St Fillan's Priory, the ruins of a small Augustinian house.

Legend has it that before the Battle of Bannockburn (on 24 June 1314) Robert the Bruce asked that the reliquary holding the arm bone of St Fillan, an Irish saint, one-time Abbot of Fife Monastery, be brought to him from Inchaffray Abbey, near Perth. The abbot, fearing

loss of the bone to the English, brought only the silver reliquary, but as he and the Bruce prayed a strange noise came from the reliquary. On opening it, the abbot discovered the bone inside. Following his victory, the Bruce endowed the house here, where St Fillan had lived out his last years. Another tale suggests the Bruce's benevolence owed more to the hospitality of the monks of the original, smaller house on the site which had sheltered him after defeat at nearby Dalrigh in 1306.

Wayfarers on the next section of the route (which recrosses the main road – take care again) may be grateful for Caulfield's efforts. Sir William Burrell, in his book on his northern horseback tour of 1758, which included parts of Scotland, rode past soldiers working on the military road our route follows and notes that when he left it 'we found ourselves in the most horrid paths that can be conceived, up and down steep hills, through bogs in some places, in others filled with large loose stones where our horses had no firm footing or, what was worse, now and then staircases of solid, craggy rock.' Of course there are those who think that the landscape Burrell describes is the very essence of wild Scotland. The way passes Dalrigh, scene of the Bruce's defeat, and then heads through Tyndrum, where gold was once mined (and accommodation is available), crossing the main road again (take care) to reach a truly magnificent piece of walking. To the right (east) here are the steep flanks of Beinn Odhar (2,955ft/901m), and then Beinn Dòrain (3,529ft/1,076m), while to the left, across the valley, are the hills above Glen Orchy.

At the base of Glen Orchy, the way crosses the river on Caulfield's Bridge of Orchy (having negotiated the main road again), climbing Màm Carraigh, and then descends to the Inveroran Hotel, where the Scottish Mountaineering Club held its earliest meets. Other guests included the poets William Wordsworth (1770–1850) and Robert Southey, and William's sister Dorothy. Dorothy was charmed by the

place, writing enthusiastically about a group of drovers who sat around a peat fire eating porridge from wooden bowls. Southey was less charmed by the 'wretched hovel'. A short distance further you cross Victoria Bridge, named for the queen when the nearby shooting lodge, Forest Lodge, was constructed.

Beyond the lodge is one of the finest sections of the walk, following the military road and a section of Thomas Telford's realignment, across the wonderful Black Mount country. To the left (west) is a rugged landscape topped by several Munros while, further on, the view east is across Rannoch Moor. The route crosses Bà Bridge, and then climbs to reach a side track to Bà Cottage. The cottage is one of many to be seen across the Highlands, a reminder of the Clearances, when crofters were forced from their holdings so that the land could be 'improved' by sheep farming. Though often depicted as a single event, the Clearances were a series of evictions, starting with (part voluntary)

ABOVE Beinn Dòrain. The route follows an old military road around the peak's base.

OPPOSITE

ABOVE The Bridge of Orchy.

BELOW Am Monadh Dubh (Black Mount) and the high peaks near Glen Etive seen across Lochan na h-Achlaise. The route across the edge of Rannoch Moor from Bridge of Orchy to Blackrock Cottage traces a line between the lochan and the peaks.

mass emigration after the Jacobite rebellions, which saw an end to the old Highland life. While it is now customary to see the Clearances as acts of appalling vandalism of both the country and Highland culture, the loss of the feudal (or, at least, semi-feudal) clan system and the crofting life can be over-romanticized. The crofter evictions were often extremely brutal and cannot be condoned, but the life of the crofter was very hard and almost certainly not one those who now rue its loss would willingly share.

The way climbs to about 1,460ft (445m), from where there is a marvellous view over Rannoch Moor, about 50 sq. miles (about 130 sq. km) of peat bog and one of the last great wildernesses of Britain. The moor, once cloaked in pine forest, long gone because of fire and logging, has had mixed reviews, varying from the shudders of horror of those crossing by stagecoach a hundred years ago to the modern walker who finds it a life-affirming, though difficult, place.

Ahead now is Buachaille Etive Mòr (3,345ft/1,022m), one of the great mountains of Scotland, even though it does not manage a place in the hundred highest Munros. The Buachaille – the name means 'great herdsman (or shepherd) of Etive' – stands at the entrances to both Glen Etive and Glencoe and forms a 5 mile (8km) ridge that includes four main summits, though it is the pyramidal form of Stob Dearg, the

ABOVE The route north from Forest Lodge skirts Rannoch Moor, but at Lochan Mhic Pheadair Ruadhe the landscape is very similar to that of the moor.

OPPOSITE Bà Bridge, one of the most famous landmarks on the route, and an ideal spot for wild camping.

ABOVE Walkers on the route near Bà Bridge.
LEFT Kingshouse Hotel.

OPPOSITE Ben Nevis, to the left of the Mamores, from the top of the Devil's Staircase.

highest peak, that is most often photographed, particularly the peak's north-east face which, with its cliffs and gullies, looks just as a mountain should.

The way descends to Blackrock Cottage – to the left from here is the Glencoe Ski Centre – turns right, crosses the main road again (take care) and follows a track to the Kingshouse Hotel. The hotel claims to be Scotland's oldest inn (though it is not the only claimant) and began life as a drove road stopover, which perhaps explains early references to it being distinctly unflattering. In 1791 a traveller noted it did not have a bed fit to sleep in and offered poor food, while in 1803 Dorothy Wordsworth was outraged. The proprietor was a 'screaming harridan', the place was 'wretched . . . as dirty as a house after a sale on a rainy day', a fire was lit only after interminable persuasion but was necessary because the bed sheets were wet, and the food was barely edible. Today's walker will be better served.

From the hotel the Buachaille dominates the view as you head for the Devil's Staircase, a persistent – though not especially steep – climb from Altnafeadh that took the military road over the pass to Kinlochleven. On the climb there is a view into Glencoe. Glencoe is both famous and infamous, the former because of its importance in the history of Scottish mountaineering, the latter because of the events of 13 February 1692. Following the Jacobite rising sparked by the crowning of William of Orange as William III, those who had supported the rebellion, chiefly the Highland clans, were offered a pardon if they swore an oath of allegiance to the new king by 1 January 1692. On 31 December 1691, Alastair MacIain, clan chief of the MacDonalds of Glencoe, travelled to Fort William to take the oath. His attempt was stalled by the governor there, who sent him to Inverary for the swearing. It was a ploy: the English government and the Scottish lowland lords were keen to see a limiting of the potential threat of the Highlanders and intent on making an example of someone. A detachment of 120 soldiers from the Earl of Argyll's Regiment led by Captain Robert Campbell was sent to Glencoe, where they were received kindly and billeted in the scattering of cottages in the valley for two weeks. Then, at 5.00 a.m. on 13 February, following orders they had received the night before, the soldiers attacked their hosts. They killed 38 or 39 men (including MacIain) and, it is believed, a further 40 women and children died of exposure when their homes were burned. The Glencoe Massacre became a byword for treachery, and was instrumental in the simmering hatred that led to the Jacobite rebellions of the fifty years which followed.

From the top of the Devil's Staircase, the highest point on the route at 1,797ft (548m), the view ahead to Ben Nevis and the Mamores is stunning. The way now descends to Kinlochleven, claimed by Bill Murray, a leading Scottish mountaineer of the second half of the last century, as the 'ugliest [village] on two thousand miles of Highland coast'. His view was, in part, coloured by the aluminium smelter, which closed in 2000, but it has to be said that even with the works gone, the place is still no scenic highlight, though the Grey Mare's Tail waterfall, a 140ft (40m) fall in a picturesque wooded glade, is worth the short detour.

From the town the way enters its final stage, a long one, as it is about 14 miles (22km) to Fort William with no food/drink stops or shelter. It starts by ascending through a fine U-shaped valley to Lairigmor, meaning 'great pass', at 1,082ft (330m). From there the way turns

north, descending through forests to reach a minor road in Glen Nevis on the outskirts of Fort William. The final walking is along the road, or its verge, into the town. The first fort here was built by Oliver Cromwell, the town being named for the fort after it was garrisoned by troops of William III in the wake of the Jacobite rumblings which greeted his coronation. The town's Gaelic name reflects its origins: An Gearasdan means 'The Garrison'. After Inverness, Fort William is the largest settlement in the Highlands and it is a centre for outdoor enthusiasts. Many arrive to climb Ben Nevis, at 4,406ft (1,343.3m) Britain's highest peak. Many of the routes to the top are serious climbing expeditions, particularly in winter, though the 'tourist trail' is much less demanding. It is, though, long and involves climbing every foot of the height as it starts at sea level. From the way, Ben Nevis is not visible, but you can obtain the classic view of the peak by a taking a short detour around Loch Linnhe to Corpach, where its (impressive, if hardly elegant) bulk can be seen looming over the town.

The classic view of Ben Nevis, from Corpach, near Fort William.

Travel

By air The airport at Glasgow is the end-point for flights by budget airlines which transfer from many UK airports. From it buses run to Glasgow or to the nearby rail station at Paisley Gilmour Street for train connections.

By rail Both Milngavie and Fort William have rail stations, allowing wayfarers to use the train to arrive from, and return to, Glasgow.

By road Milngavie is easily reached over the Erskine Bridge from the M8 motorway, which links to Glasgow and the M74 as well as other major Scottish lowland roads. Fort William is well served by roads to/from Inverness and Glasgow.

Maps and guides

The West Highland Way, Bob Aitken and Roger Smith, Mercat Press (the official Scottish Natural Heritage guide, including a Harveys map of the route).
West Highland Way, Charlie Loram, Trailblazer Publications.
Both are excellent; Loram's is newer (published 2008). There are also several other good guides.

Harveys produces a hard-wearing polyethlene map covering the entire route at 1:40,000 for walkers who do not get the official guide (and, therefore, a free copy). Those using Ordnance Survey 1:50,000 maps will need five sheets: 64, 57, 56, 50 and 41. Explorer (1:25,000) maps are, of course, also available: sheets 348, 347, 364, 377, 384 and 392 are needed.

Waymarking

Good throughout, using a standard symbol of a white thistle within a hexagon. The direction of the route is also signed with a yellow arrow.

Accommodation

There is a full range, from camping, which is ideal in the wilderness areas, through bothies to bed and breakfasts and hotels. The way can be staged so as to make camping unnecessary, only the final stage to Fort William being long.

Equipment

Full wet/windy-weather gear is essential as the Scottish mountains are notorious for producing bad weather quickly. Warm clothing is also essential, as it can be surprisingly chilly on the route, even in summer. In the main, the tracks the route follows are good, but some sections are rough, so good footwear is also essential.

Climate

Highland summers are warm, but not hot, while winters are cold with precipitation which once fell as snow and gave Scottish winter climbing an enviable reputation. Increasingly it is rain that falls in early and late winter, which is much less fun. Summer has long days (up to eighteen hours daily), but spring flowers and autumn colours are delightful.

Hazards

Summer brings long, warm days, but also midges: biting insects of the genus Culicoides, the most ferocious of which is the Highland biting midge, *C. impunctatus*. The female of the species needs a blood meal to form eggs. When feeding she releases a chemical that informs her numerous friends that she has found a suitable host. Midges swarm from mid-May to the end of August, but the exact timing is variable and some years appear worse than others. The bite is usually only mildly irritating, but with enough bites . . .

Horse flies (called clegs in Scotland) are also a nuisance in early summer. The common Scottish species is *Haematopota pluvialis*, but there are other British horse flies. The bite is unpleasant, and many people react badly to them.

Finally, the famed Scottish Six-Day Motor Cycle Trials, held in early May each year, often use sections of the old military road around Bridge of Orchy.

National Parks and Wildlife

The way lies within the Loch Lomond and Trossachs National Park from south of Drymen to a point just north of Tyndrum. Covering an area of 720 sq. miles (1,865 sq. km), the park scenery ranges from sea lochs where seals and porpoises swim (and otters are seen on the shoreline), and forested areas which are home to red squirrel, roe and fallow deer, and a host of woodland birds, to open mountain where red deer are seen. The park's uplands include twenty Munros. In winter Arctic breeding geese and whooper swans take up residence, while resident birds include capercaillie and black grouse.

The way also passes through the old oak forest of Mugdock, where the plant life includes yellow tormentil, blue milkwort, scabious and the insectivorous butterwort. The bay area of the Loch Lomond Nature Reserve is the overwintering site for white-fronted and greylag geese arriving from Greenland. In summer, ospreys fish the bay waters. In spring Inchcailloch Island is famous for its bluebells, ramsons (wild garlic) and primroses. There are also wood sorrel and other woodland species. The island's oaks are home to many bird species, including wood warblers, crossbills, redstarts and goldcrests.

The nearby island of Inchconnachan is equally famous for its herd of red-necked wallaby. The animals were introduced in the early twentieth century by Lady Colquhoun and have recently been the subject of controversy: some people want them culled as they are a perceived threat to the capercaillie population, while others see such a cull as an abuse of animal rights, and point out that the wallabies are popular with tourists.

North of the National Park summer visitors will become familiar with heather (actually several different species), on which red grouse feed, while searching the skyline for red deer and the sky for golden eagles. Look out, too, for butterflies. The way passes through areas where it is possible to see mountain argus, mountain ringlet and the rare chequered skipper, the entire British population of which is found in Lochaber and nearby north Argyll.

ABOVE Red deer stag.
RIGHT Highland cow. Most Highland cattle are red-brown, but this animal is a much more interesting colour.

OPPOSITE
ABOVE LEFT Cuckoo flower.
ABOVE RIGHT Dog violet.
BELOW Golden eagle.

Inaccessible Pinnacle

ISLE OF SKYE, SCOTLAND

Skye is the second largest of the islands off Scotland's western coast, but very much the most romantic for its beautiful name and the famous song recording the escape of the Jacobite rebel Bonnie Prince Charlie, with the aid of Flora MacDonald and a small boat. For walkers, Skye is equally famous for the Cuillins, though these peaks are more the playground of the climber/mountaineer than the average hillwalker, as they are spiky and intimidating, difficult to ascend and navigate, and include one that can only be reached by an exposed rock climb.

Geologically Skye is an open-air lesson in rock forms. Though there are sedimentary rocks, most of the island is basalt, a layer up to 6,500ft (2,000m) thick having been deposited by Tertiary volcanoes. But in the south of the island, differential erosion has exposed the roots of those ancient volcanoes, and the reddish granite which forms the Red Hills and the dark gabbro which forms the Cuillins. The Cuillins are named An Cuiltheann in Gaelic, perhaps for the mythological hero Cúchulainn, who is said to have learned his fighting at a school on the island.

The twelve Munros of the Cuillins (eleven on the main ridge and one an outlier) have long attracted Munro-baggers (see page 221), while traversing the main ridge, taking in all eleven main peaks, is an aspiration for many mountaineers. Gabbro is a rough rock, which aids the climber, making the scrambling necessary to reach the tops straightforward even in damp conditions, though there is still a surprising amount of loose rock, which calls for caution. However, the one Munro that requires rock climbing, the Inaccessible Pinnacle

OPPOSITE The view into Glen Brittle from the ascent route.

BELOW Sgurr Dearg and the Inaccessible Pinnacle.

(known by almost all climbers as InPin), is basalt, which is much more slippery in the wet. The climbing itself is relatively easy, with only one move of any difficulty before you reach the summit, but the big drops on each side make it a daunting climb.

The ascent of InPin starts from Glen Brittle, where an ad hoc car park for half-a-dozen cars lies close to the Memorial Hut (owned jointly by the British and Scottish Mountaineering Councils). From here, head towards the sheep pens; then cross the bridge and follow the clear path uphill to the Eas Mor (Great Waterfall), which drops 80ft (25m) into a pool set within a mountain hollow, an exquisite place. Ahead now the path forks: bear left (the right-hand fork is the return route). Follow the path into Coire na Banachdich where, eventually, it is lost among the boulders and scree. Cairns aid walkers here, but they may be hard to follow even in good weather. The going is not too difficult, however, and numerous routes can be forged to the high ridge above, though the steep scree gullies of some of these can be very intimidating. Eventually you reach Bealach Coire na Banachdich (2,792ft/851m), the low point on the ridge between the Munros of Sgurr na Banachdich (3,165ft/965m), to the north, and Sgurr Dearg, our objective, to the right.

As you bear right on a path up the scree-covered slope of the peak, InPin eventually appears above the ridge crest. Walkers, particularly those with limited climbing experience, have to settle for a view of the pinnacle from Sgurr Dearg (3,208ft/978m). Solo experienced climbers should do the same, but parties can now climb the pinnacle, the usual route being along the 150ft (50m) fin-like East Ridge, which is graded Moderate. The shorter (65ft/20m) West Ridge, graded Very Difficult,

is the usual descent line, climbers abseiling down it. The pinnacle (3,234ft/986m) was first climbed in 1880 by Charles and Lawrence Pilkington. Interestingly, Sir Hugh Munro, the first to tabulate the 3,000ft (914.6m) peaks which now bear his name, never climbed it, and actually listed it as a subsidiary top of Sgurr Dearg, despite noting, correctly, that it is higher. At present 283 Munros are recognized, those seeking to climb them all occasionally being called Munro-baggers.

From the pinnacle, you can reverse the outward route, but better is to follow the ramp below the pinnacle's south face and then continue around the head of Coire Lagan. South of the traverse there are steep cliffs, so you have to be patient, continuing until a steep scree path leads down into the corrie. Bear right at a path fork to follow the edge of Loch an Fhir-bhallaich (the Lake of the Speckled Trout), continuing to the fork reached on the outward journey. Now reverse the outward route.

Walk information

Map: Ordnance Survey 1:25,000 (Explorer) sheet 411. Start/finish: Glen Brittle Memorial Hut. Length: 5 miles (8km). Ascent: 3,300ft (1,010m).

BELOW Eas Mor waterfall. Beyond it is Coire na Banachdich, with the Sgurr Dearg ridge on the right skyline.

OPPOSITE The magnificent, but uncompromising, country crossed on the ascent.

Kungsleden

SWEDEN

About 400 million years ago the activity of tectonic plates created the Caledonian Mountains, which stretched from North America to Europe. The remnants of these peaks, eroded by the passage of time and ice, can still be seen in the Appalachians, Greenland and Scotland, and in Scandinavia, where they are known as the Scandes. These form the backbone of Norway, where the highest peaks are found, and smaller, lower blocks in northern Sweden, where the tallest mountains are north of the Arctic Circle. Erosion and glaciation have sculpted these, creating the beautiful, jagged scenery of the Sarek National Park and the superb alpine scenery around Kebnekaise, Sweden's highest mountain.

The exact height of Kebnekaise is debated. The north summit has a limited burden of permanent snow and includes solid ground at 6,878ft/2,097m; the southern summit is snow-capped, its height varying with the season. Figures as high as 6,944ft/2,117m are occasionally cited, but 6,901ft/2,104m is the official height.

Kebnekaise is made of black, mafic (ferromagnesian) rock. The outcropping of rich iron ore to the east of the peak, at Kiruna, might be expected to originate from a similar source, but is in fact much older, the ore body having been formed 1,600 million years ago by intense volcanic activity. The Kiruna ore body (a magnetite-apatite mix with an iron content of 60 per cent) originally held 1,800 million tons (the present reserve is about 675 million tons) and is the main reason why Sweden, a small and – in European terms – relatively non-industrialized country, has been able to support two car manufacturers (Saab and Volvo). Today the ore is shipped by rail from Kiruna to Narvik for export.

The railway line can also be used to reach Abisko, a tiny hamlet close to the Norwegian border, which is the starting point of one of Europe's finest long-distance trails. Kungsleden, or the Royal Trail, as it is now called, has a long history, as the occasionally conflicting desires of Sámi farmers/herders and the Svenska Turistföreningen (STF), a charitable organization committed to encouraging access to the Swedish wilderness, meant that it was almost a hundred years from initial concept to the creation of an official, waymarked path.

At 260 miles (420km) and about 25,000ft (7,600m) of climbing, Kungsleden is a major undertaking, but the reward is a walk through magnificent scenery in a country with a very different cultural heritage from that of the more southern landscapes covered in this book. This is Sámi country – Sámi now being the preferred name for the people originally called Lapps. Walkers will visit few Sámi settlements, but will brush past them for most of the journey.

OPPOSITE
ABOVE On the *spongs* (boardwalks) of the early part of the route in the Abisko National Park.
BELOW The Abisko River canyon.

BELOW Checking the weight of a rucsac at the Abisko fjellstation before setting off along Kungsleden.

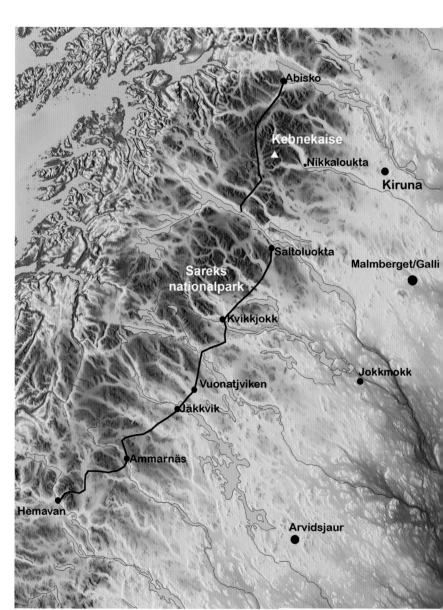

In his guide to the route, Claes Grundsten – one of Sweden's foremost wilderness photographers – says it is best to walk Kungsleden north–south so that the sun warms the face. At the height of summer, of course, the sun never leaves the sky above the Arctic Circle, and about 60 per cent of this route lies north of the Circle, but it is a fair point, and invariably walkers do head south, as we do here.

Beautifully sited beside Lake Torneträsk, Abisko is little more than a fjellstation, the Swedish equivalent of the mountain refuge of the European Alps. The one at Abisko is huge, with 300 beds, a fine restaurant and shops for both food and equipment. To reach the arch that is the official start of the route, you must cross the road, go under the railway line and bear right. From the first step of the walk you are in the Abisko National Park, an area of mountain taiga, as this landscape of valley forest and alpine upland is called.

The walk starts beside a rocky canyon of the Abisko River, and then uses boardwalks and bridges to keep the walker dry-shod on the journey to Abeskojárvi Lake. Follow the lake's eastern edge, with the steep wall of Giron (5,087ft/1,551m) to the left, to reach Abiskojaure, the first STF hut along the route.

On this first stage, Kungsleden shares its path for a short distance with the Dag Hammarskjöld Way, named for the Swedish diplomat who was the second Secretary-General of the United Nations, and widely considered one of the finest to have held the post: John F. Kennedy called him 'the greatest statesman of our century'.

RIGHT Looking north along the valley near Kaitumjaure. Here again the route threads through a landscape ideal for wildlife.

OPPOSITE
ABOVE Aerial view of the northern section of the route from the east. In the background is the lake of Alisjárvi with the scattered huts of a Sámi settlement on its eastern (near) shore. On the top of the hill in the foreground is an ancient Sámi reindeer enclosure.
BELOW When spring melts winter's snows and the top layer of the permafrost, plant life erupts in numerous shades of green. This aerial shot shows the country near Sälkastugorna, where the route follows *spongs* through boggy country which is an ideal habitat for wildlife, particularly birds.

Hammarskjöld (1905–61) was killed in an aircraft crash; he was awarded the Nobel Peace Prize posthumously, and is now regarded as a leading Christian mystic. The way has many meditation points along its route.

From the Abiskojaure fjellstation, Kungsleden leaves lush birch forest for open country, following a wide valley dotted with lakes, which are the feeding and breeding ground of waterfowl. The valley narrows as you progress, passing the fjellstation of Alesjaure and then climbing to reach that at Tjäktja. The climb continues, reaching a pass at about 3,600ft (1,100m), from where the view opens up to the east and south. South is Tjäktjajåkka, the long, gently curving valley of the Tjäktja River, while to the east are the high peaks around Kebnekaise. Kungsleden descends gently to the fjellstation at Sälka and then descends further, over undulating ground, to that at Singi.

The Singi fjellstation is a popular overnight stop for walkers completing only the first four or five days of Kungsleden before heading east to Nikkaluokta and a bus for Kiruna. They invariably use the Kebnekaise fjellstation as a halfway stopover, sharing the accommodation with those climbing the peak. The climb of Kebnekaise is long, but not technically difficult. A good day is needed, however, as mist on the highest ground can cause route-finding problems; there are emergency huts close to the summit, and posts from them lead the way to the top. From the summit the view is astounding: it is claimed that from Kebnekaise's southern (higher) summit you can see 15,500 sq. miles (40,000 sq. km), representing some 8 per cent of the total area of Sweden. To the south, the view extends to the Sarek peaks.

Kungsleden continues south through majestic Tjäktjajåkka towards the Kaitum fjellstation. Along the way, the open landscape after the tighter section of valley between the peaks of Stuor Avrrik (4,441ft/1,354m), to the right, and Stuor Jiertá (5,061ft/1,543m), to the left, is an open-air geomorphology lesson. Here the retreating

ABOVE The Rabots Glacier and Kebnekaise from the west.
LEFT Teusajaure (Teusa Lake). The first boat crossing on the route is from the fjellstation which can be seen near the spit of land.

OPPOSITE
ABOVE Cloud-shrouded hillside on the descent to Vakkotavare.
BELOW Passengers joining the ferry for Saltoluokta on a damp day.

glacier which carved the valley has left mounds known as kames. These are formed when streams flowing beneath glaciers form channels in the ice, which eventually silt up with glacial till. When the glacier retreats, the long, sinuous till ridges are left behind as eskers. Beyond the glacial snout eskers may be broken by stream action, forming mounds, and occasionally steep cones. Look out for these kames as you head south to reach the fjellstation on the northern shore of Kaitumjaure (Lake Kaitum). From the huts there is a short stage that crosses the Sjaunja Nature Reserve, a botanical reserve set up to protect bog-loving species such as the rare bog rosemary, and ends at the Teusajaure fjellstation.

Here one of the delights of the Royal Trail awaits: the walk continues on the other side of the lake, after a 1,000yd (1km) boat crossing. There are three rowing boats, but if you find there is only one on your side, you will need to row across three times to ensure that at least one boat is available on each shore. Solo walkers will need to tow a boat back on one of their journeys. The rowing is fun, but hard work, especially if a strong wind is funnelling through the tight gorge that the lake fills. If the station warden is on site, he may take you across in his motor boat (for a small fee). If not, you will have to row. The mid-point of the lake is a boundary of the Stora Sjöfallets National Park.

Back on dry land, the route traverses the park with a long, steep climb that necessitates crossing a couple of streams, which can be difficult after heavy rain, though the widest of the streams now has a bridge. Beyond the high point (at about 2,950ft/900m) the descent crosses several more streams and then steepens considerably. Ahead are the peaks of the Sarek, while close by there is a view of the vast south-

western face of Garńńjelabákte, which drops almost vertically 4,250ft (1,300m) into Suorvajaure. There is a fjellstation (Vakkotavare) beside the lake, and you can take a bus from here to avoid walking 20 miles (32km) along the lakeside road. The bus connects with a ferry at Kebnats, which whisks you across Suorvajaure to Saltoluokta, the next fjellstation. The real name of the site is Kaltoluokta (bay with a spring), but the cartographer working on the first map of the area had poor handwriting and his 'k' was interpreted as an 's'. The place has been Saltoluokta ever since.

While on the ferry, you leave the Stora Sjöfallets National Park, though its boundary is only a short distance to the west. The walk now runs parallel to the eastern boundary of the Sarek National Park, one of the finest mountain wildernesses in Europe. Though the walk south is occasionally hemmed in by forest, and the view foreshortened by peaks to the west, there are occasional fine views across the Sarek's impressive range. Though lower than Kebnekaise, the high Sareks are sensational.

The walk from Saltoluokta ends at the fjellstation beside Sitojaure, close to the Sámi settlement Vággevárási. You can visit the settlement: indeed it is almost essential to do so, as the Sámi run the ferry across the lake. It is possible to row across, but here the distance is 2.5 miles

(4km) which, if three journeys are required, is a long, long way, particularly if the water is choppy. By contrast the Sámi motorboat takes only half an hour to reach Svine, where cloudberries grow. Cloudberries are a delicacy to both Norwegians and Swedes, who walk great distances to gather them. Most Scandinavian restaurants offer the berries as part of a dessert, perhaps with waffles, ice cream or cream, that is both highly prized and highly priced. All matters of taste are, of course, personal, but the berries always seem overvalued to me, the taste ordinary in comparison to that of fresh strawberries or raspberries. If time permits, seek out some fresh berries to make your own judgement.

You now climb through birch forest to open ground and a fine view north. Ahead, the eye is soon drawn to the next lake, Laitaure, and the delta of the Rapa River, flowing down from the Sarek at its western end. From Aktse, the fjellstation at the lake shore, the view is dominated by the vast cliff face of Skierffe (3,867ft/1,179m), which hangs over the Rapa delta. At the base of the cliff is a cave, once a Sámi ritual site.

You must now cross the lake by rowing or motor boat – and the view towards the Sarek from mid-lake is superb. Back on land, forest walking again gives way to open fell, the view left (south) taking in

RIGHT The dining room of the fjellstation at Kvikkjokk.
BELOW In the Pieljekaise National Park. Looking north towards Sädvajarue lake. In the foreground is a Kungsleden waymarker.

OPPOSITE Hornavan Lake near Jäkkvik. The lake was once crossed by boat, but the route now meanders around its northern and western shores to reach the Jäkkvik fjellstation.

ABOVE Syterskalet from the east, with Norra Sytertoppen on the right.

Tjaktjaure, a lake whose size was increased massively when it was dammed. The flooding of much of the valley in which the original lake sat is the largest act of landscape alteration ever in Sweden and was highly controversial, though the enlarged lake has had much less impact on the environment than was feared by many protesters. You soon reach the Pårte fjellstation, from where a low-level walk through forest and bogland leads you to Kvikkjokk, only the second point at which you see a road on the journey from Abisko. There is another lake to be crossed here, Lake Sakkat; a regular ferry plies from a jetty beside it.

From the small settlement of Mallenjarka on the far side, Kungsleden climbs steadily through spruce and then birch forest, which is home to lynx, wolf, wolverine and brown bear. Each animal is elusive, and bears are also now few in number, so you are more likely to see traces than the animals themselves. At Tsielekjåhkå there is a hut, but it has just a couple of bunks and no cooking equipment. The next stages of the walk are equally poorly served by fjellstations at present: the whole section of Kungsleden from Kvikkjokk to Vuonatjviken requires walkers to be entirely self-sufficient. For some, that is a considerable challenge in a truly wild area, but for others it is the very essence of long-distance trekking.

From Tsielekjåhkå, Kungsleden climbs to open fell, crossing a bridge below the impressive cliff of Goabddábakte (4,152ft/1,266m) and then descending to thread its way through forest dotted with lakes, one of which (Gistojávrátj) is a beautiful spot to spend the night. Now the trail climbs steadily again to open fell, the wild, sloping plateau of Barturtte, from where you descend to the tiny hamlet of Vuonatjviken, crossing the Arctic Circle. At Vuonatjviken there is a restaurant and the possibility of hiring a self-catering hut. The hamlet stands on the northern shore of the vast Riebnes Lake, the long crossing of which definitely requires a ferry, which can be booked locally. Ask, too, about crossing Hornavan, the next lake. Kungsleden used to cross Hornavan directly to Jäkkvik, but a couple of years ago the ferry from Saudat ceased and a detour to the west was introduced, which includes a short crossing by rowing boat. It may still be possible to book a ferry from Saudat across the Hornavan in Vuonatjviken: if it is, it may be worth contemplating, as it is only a short walk (perhaps two hours) from the southern edge of Riebnes to Saudat, and then a short ferry ride to the heady delights of the Jäkkvik fjellstation.

Jäkkvik is on Route 95, an important road which links Arvidsjaur with Norway, though you are unlikely to have to dodge much traffic to continue the walk, climbing through beautiful woodland alive with flowers in spring. On entering the Pieljekaise National Park there is open fell, with wonderful views to the north and west. Beyond a pass – where the peak of Pieljekaise (3,729ft/1,137m), which gives its name to the park, lies to the left (east) – you reach an overnight hut. There is a gas stove here, as well as a vast elk antler rack, with nineteen points: the bull was killed by a rival near by during the annual rut. From the hut, you continue downhill, and then bear left to pass around the southern tip of Luvtávrre.

The route now descends through forest to reach Adolfsström, a village that owes its existence to silver ore found locally. With abundant timber for the production of charcoal, the silver smelter built here seemed destined for wealth and importance, but in practice silver production never reached the expected levels and the village was all but abandoned after some forty years. Today the few villagers make a living from visitors and limited agriculture.

To shorten the walk by about 5 miles (8km) from the village it is possible to organize a boat trip to the western tip of Iraft Lake. The walk from there is across more empty country, so you must be self-sufficient again as you cross fell where once, before global warming, snowy owls bred regularly. Their chief prey, lemming, need stable snow covering to provide insulation, as they do not hibernate; rain and poor snow have reduced their winter survival. Consequently snowy owls have not bred in any part of Scandinavia for several years. Arctic fox and long-tailed skua also feed on lemming, so the decline of their population has affected their numbers too. As Sweden warms, red foxes spread north: being bigger than their Arctic cousins, they out-compete them, and force the smaller animals ever northward.

You may need to spend two nights camping before you reach Ammarnäs, though you can pass the second in the hut at Rävfjallet, where there is a kitchen. Ammarnäs is the largest settlement on Kungsleden (though the terminal village of Hemavan is about the same size). It is a pretty place, with a collection of stilted houses close to the church which are occupied by local Sámi when they visit town, particularly for church services. Both accommodation and meals are available here. From the village the walk goes south, and then turns west; you can use the basic huts at Servestugan to overnight before reaching Tärnasjön Lake and another basic hut. The route follows the lake shore south, then crosses bridges to islets close to the lake's southern tip to reach the final, glorious section of walking.

From the Syterstugan fjellstation, the first real mountain refuge for many kilometres, Kungsleden follows Syterskalet, a near-perfect U-shaped valley which opens up between Norra Sytertoppen (5,799ft/1,768m) and Södra Sytertoppen (5,527ft/1,685m), the high peaks of the Norra Storfjället massif. The valley is almost straight for 2 miles (3km) and then arcs left and broadens. Here is another fjellstation, popular with walkers exploring the high peaks and their tiny glaciers. From the hut it is a short walk of about 7 miles (11km) to Hemavan.

ABOVE Young reindeer.

OPPOSITE The start (or finish) of Kungsleden at Abisko.

Travel

By air Kiruna is the closest airport to Abisko, which you can reach by rail. The closest airport to Hemavan is at Arvidsjaur, but that still leaves a long rail and/or road journey.

By rail Trains link Abisko to Stockholm for those wishing to avoid the flight to Kiruna. Storuman can be reached by rail, and from there buses run to Hemavan.

By road Both Abisko and Hemavan are served by good roads, but the location of the walk – straddling the Arctic Circle – means that the start and end points, and all points between, are remote.

Maps and guides

Kungsleden: The Royal Trail through Arctic Sweden, Claes Grundsten, Carreg Ltd.
This is a splendid guide to the route, translated from the Swedish original.

Lantmäteriet, the Swedish Ordnance Survey, publishes a full set of maps of Sweden. For Kungsleden the best are those at 1:100,000. That is a large scale for a walking map, but it is adequate, as for much of the route's length the way is clear on the ground. The following maps are required: BD6, BD8, BD10, BD14, BD16 and AC2.

The naming of peaks, settlements, etc. in northern Sweden can cause problems as there are usually both Swedish and Sámi versions, and as the latter has several dialects, that can mean even more versions. Here I have used the names as given on the Lantmäteriet maps.

Waymarking

In general, this is reasonable throughout. Though often short of signage, the path is very distinct on the ground, particularly in the northern section, where duckboards in boggier areas and a well-trodden path mean it is difficult to get off route. In the south there are areas where signage and paths could be improved, but given good visibility the walker will rarely be troubled. Waymarking is usually by conventional signpost, and often seen only at path junctions.

Accommodation

It is not possible to walk Kungsleden relying solely on fjellstations, though the more popular sections (the northern and southern ends, and Saltoluokta-Kvikkjokk) have well-sited huts. Elsewhere, walkers must be self-sufficient, using unmanned, basic huts where available, but being ready to use a tent if bad weather causes delays. The huts at Pieljekaise and Ravfallet have locked bunkrooms, a key being obtainable at Jäkkvik or Adolfsström, and returned vice versa.

Equipment

This is a serious walk through serious country and you must carry full wet/wind gear. That said, it is possible to have wonderful sunny days when lightweight clothing is all you need. For a full traverse, camping equipment is essential.

Climate

Warm, sunny days in summer are one of the great joys – and pleasant surprises – of Arctic travel. However, summer storms do occur, bringing sudden drops in temperature and chilling winds. Snowstorms are uncommon, but not unheard of either. Spring and autumn are beautiful for their flowers and colours respectively, but the route is officially closed from late autumn to early spring, as snow may make travel not only arduous but dangerous. Remember that in the Arctic, spring is in June (and the route is often unfit for travel until late June), while autumn is in September. Most walkers travel in July/August.

Hazards

The climate is a major consideration for walkers, particularly if a full traverse is contemplated. Just as unpleasant as a summer storm are the biting insects, midges and mosquitoes, which are at their worst in July and August. Rivers have to be crossed along the way: the sizeable ones are now bridged, but even smaller ones, early in the season or after rain, can be hazardous. If in doubt, turn back. Although you walk through country inhabited by bear, lynx and wolf, there are few of each and you are very unlikely to encounter one. Only bears are truly dangerous: in thick forest, making a noise will usually alert the bear to your presence and it will move away. Elk can be very dangerous if you get between a female and calf.

National Parks and Wildlife

The 29 sq. mile (75sq. km) Abisko National Park was established in 1909 to protect an important area of mountain taiga, with birch and grey alder in the valley giving way to conifers on higher ground. Crowberry and bilberry (or blueberry,) are among the shrubs. Mountain avens and moss campion may be seen on the fells, while alpine gentian, angelica and several orchids (including small white) may be seen in the valleys. Bird life includes bluethroat, Lapland bunting, ptarmigan and red-necked phalarope, and white-tailed eagle may occasionally be seen. Mammals include mountain hare and elk.

The Stora Sjöfallets National Park covers 500 sq. miles (1,278sq. km) and has a similar upland flora, with several delightful additions such as roseroot and alpine bartsia. Birds include Lapland bunting, long-tailed skua, willow grouse and the rare gyrfalcon. The mammal that walkers are most likely to see is the reindeer. Kungsleden passes close to the eastern part of the Sarek National Park, a marvellous 600 sq. miles (1,970 sq. km) of superb mountain scenery with a similar collection of flora and fauna.

The Pieljekaise National Park is tiny, covering only about 5 sq. miles (15 sq. km) into which is packed an array of flowers, including the beautiful globeflower, rare species such as alpine meadow-rue and fragrant orchid. Elk and reindeer are seen frequently here, as are golden eagle and golden plover.

Elsewhere ringed plover may be seen on the northern route; northern pintail, wigeon, tufted duck and red-throated diver frequent the numerous lakes, with dunlin working the shoreline. Look out, too, for lichen, especially reindeer moss (Cladonia lichen, not a moss despite the name) and map lichen, their profusion a testament to the pure Arctic air.

TOP Male elk.
ABOVE Red-throated diver.
RIGHT Melancholy thistle.

OPPOSITE
LEFT Bluethroat.
RIGHT ABOVE Crowberry and dwarf cornel.
RIGHT BELOW Alpine saw-wort.

INDEX

Acknowledgments

Walking can be, and for me occasionally is, a solitary occupation. But the companionship of the trail is one (among many) of the reasons we walk. Thanks are due to those who, over the years, have been willing to share the path with me and my foibles. There have been many, but the following cannot be ignored – Kev Bassindale, Per Michelsen, Tony Oliver, Mike Rogers, and Nathan Sale. One or two of them have even been good enough to lend me a photograph. Specific mention must also be made of those whose expertise and enthusiasm has raised my enjoyment of particular walks (and again have occasionally offered a photograph) – Terry Twigg (HRP, GR5, GR20, Peyrepertuse), Ken Hathaway (HRP, GR5, Ridgeway), Ian and Peter Mitchell (Stubai Horseshoe), Claes Grundsten (Kungsleden), Denise Andre (GR20), Martin Strahm (Jungfrau Horseshoe), Franza and Valeria Bonatta (AV2), Patrick Jost (Via Alpina), and to the following for use of their superb photographs: Alex Auer (mouflon), Bayerische Schlösserverwaltung (Neuschwanstein Castle), Jean Bienvenu (kri-kri), Jiri Bohdal (griffon vulture), Hanne and Jens Eriksen (alpine marmot), Dick Forsman (lammergeier), Nicklas Jarméus (martagon lily), and Lubos Mraz (fire salamander).

I thank Reinhold Schmuck for his friendship and hospitality, and for both his brilliance in flying the helicopter and his patience in tolerating my requests for the craft to be manoeuvred into difficult positions.

Finally I thank my wife Susan for her unerring enthusiasm for both the project and the hills. Most of the shots on the Mürren *klettersteig* are of her, its difficulties and exposure seriously challenging her nerve. It is to her enormous credit that she completed the traverse and that our marriage survived.